Edward Burne-Jones
THE PERSEUS SERIES

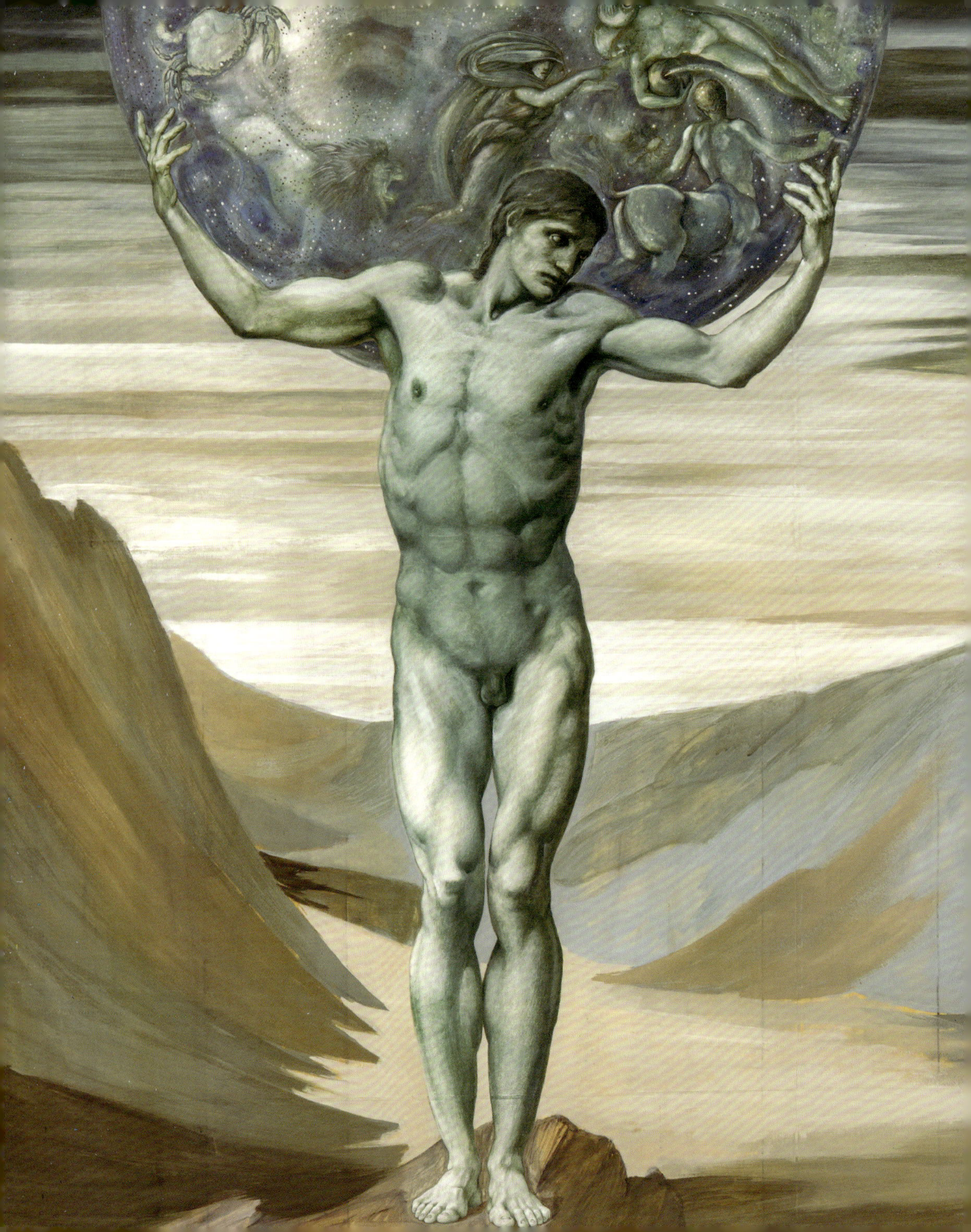

Edward Burne-Jones
THE PERSEUS SERIES

Anne Anderson and Michael Cassin

SOUTHAMPTON
CITY ART GALLERY

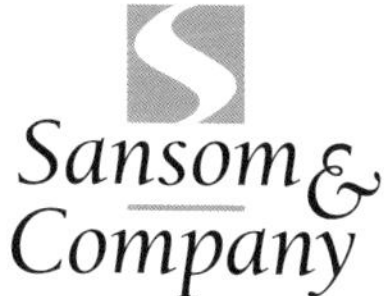

Sansom &
Company

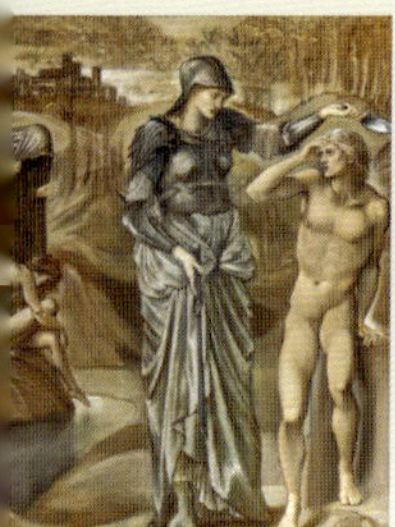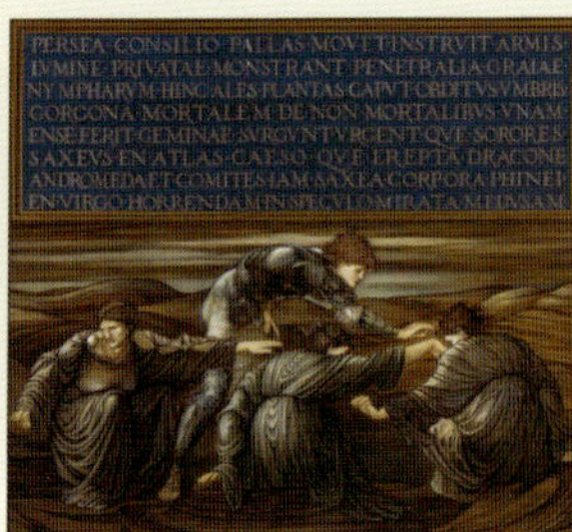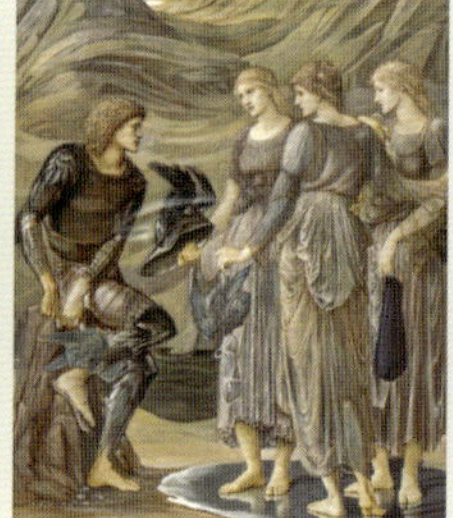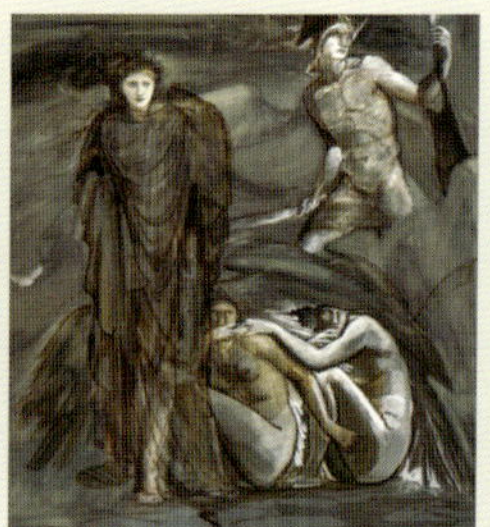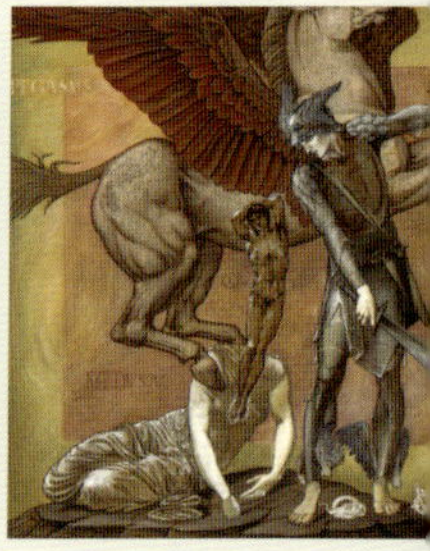

First published in 2018 by Sansom and Company,
a publishing imprint of Redcliffe Press Ltd.,
81G Pembroke Road, Bristol BS8 3EA

www.sansomandcompany.co.uk
info@sansomandcompany.co.uk

This book has been made possible with the support of

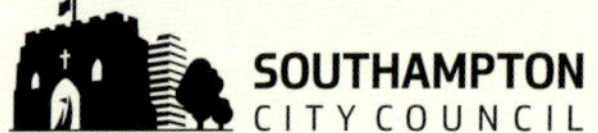

Text: © Anne Anderson and Michael Cassin 2018
Photography of *The Perseus Series*: © Southampton City Art Gallery 2018

ISBN 978-1-911408-37-6

British Library Cataloguing-in-Publication Data
A catalogue record for this book is available from the British Library.

Design and typesetting by E&P Design
Photography of *The Perseus Series* by Paul Carter

Printed and bound by Zenith Media

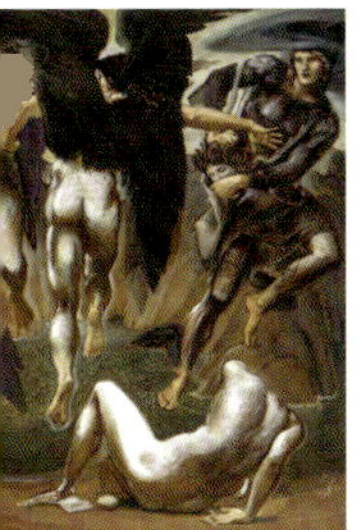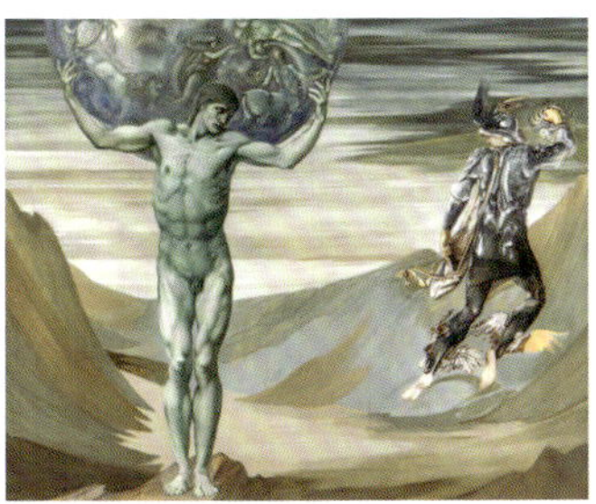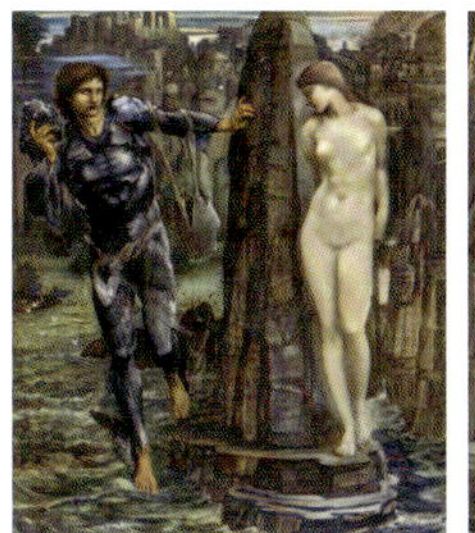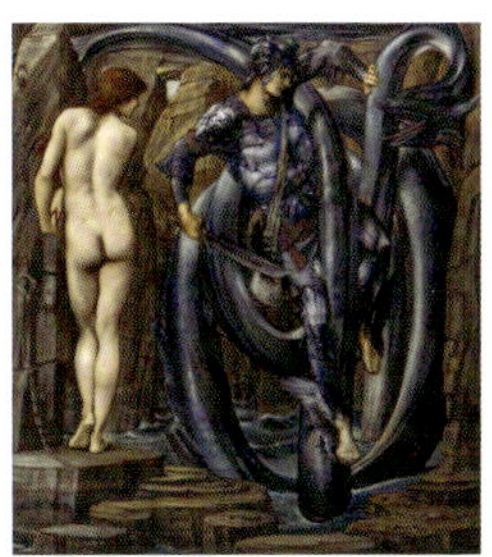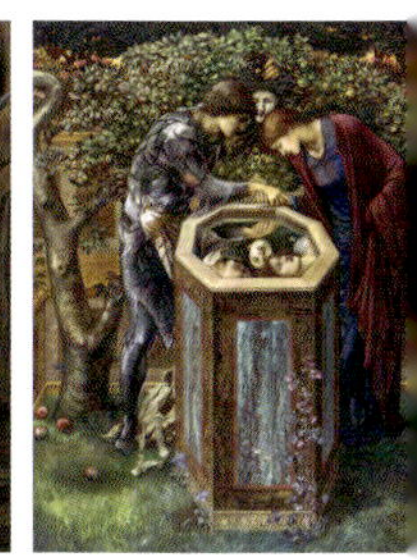

A Painter of Souls

The Perseus Story

A Painter of Souls

Anne Anderson

I mean by a picture a beautiful, romantic dream of something that never was, never will be – in a light better than any light that ever shone – in a land no one can define or remember, only desire – and the forms divinely beautiful – and then I wake up.[1]

As many artists opted to paint modern life, recording both the social habits and dress of later Victorian society, the art of Sir Edward Coley Burne-Jones, 1st Baronet ARA (1833–98) has inevitably been cast as escapist.[2] It appears both the artist and his audience wished to avoid the harsh realities of everyday life.[3] Burne-Jones, the dreamer and visionary, retreated into an imaginary world where beauty rules supreme. This world is peopled not with the living but with beautiful souls. Burne-Jones attempted to recapture a lost heroic past, when knights rescued damsels in distress or pursued a long and arduous quest.[4] His world could be in the past, with its references to both classical myths and medieval legends but essentially it is timeless, like 'some other place of being'.[5] In his essay of 1883 John Ruskin recognised Burne-Jones as a painter of mythology and personification, his figures representing 'only general truths or abstract ideas'.[6] He created a mythical world in order to explore the meaning and purpose of life. You did not go to Burne-Jones for naturalism or realism; his paintings appealed to an intellectual elite who were prepared to grapple with complex ideas.

Yet Burne-Jones achieved a popular appeal which he has maintained to this day. By 1900 he was linked to a certain brand of Englishness that embraced medieval chivalry and was exemplified in the pseudo-Elizabethan mansion created by Sir Edwin Lutyens to house the Morris and Co. exhibit at the Paris Universal Exposition. With its preoccupation with Arthurian legends and the Quest for the Holy Grail, his art became associated with establishment values: duty, honour and courage. These

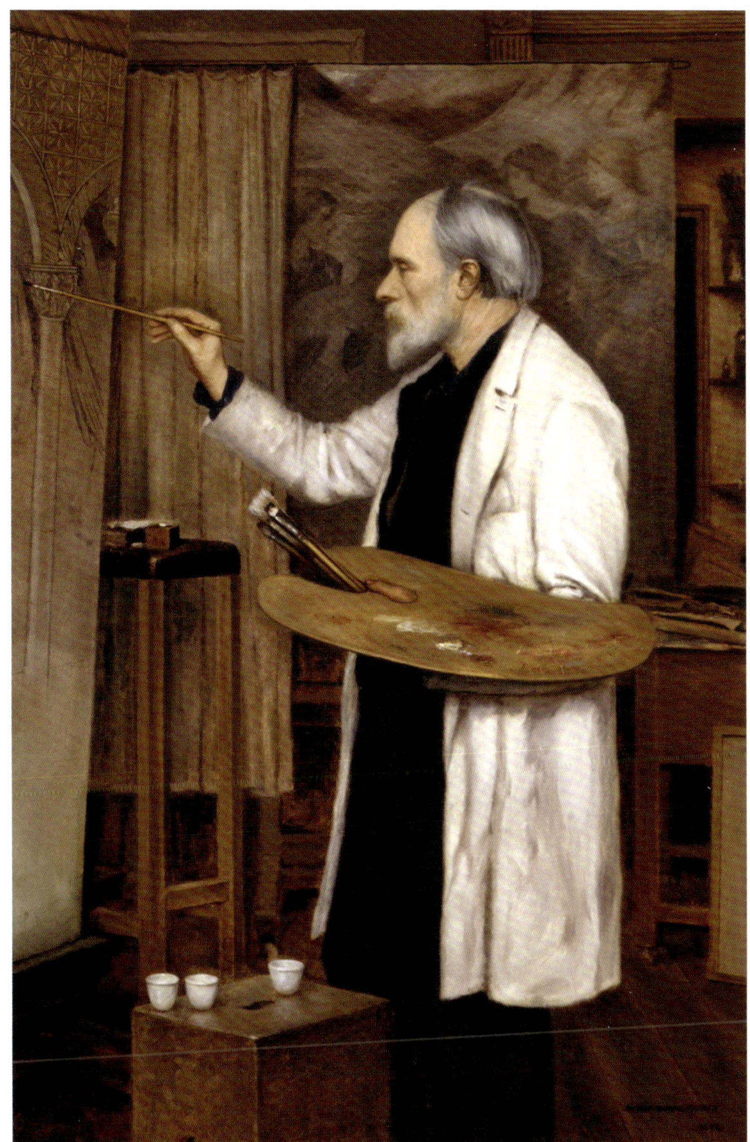

FIG. 1

Sir Edward Burne-Jones by Sir Philip Burne-Jones, 2nd Bt, 1898, oil on canvas

© National Portrait Gallery, London

values would be hard pressed with the onslaught of the First World War.

Of course his world is not easy for us to understand. At first sight it is rather rarefied and precious, remote and even irrelevant to our lives. His paintings require us to think, as they are not instantly comprehended. The images are frequently ambiguous, with much of the interpretation left to the viewer. It is this that makes his images so intriguing, while his uncertainty shows a human side which endears him to us. As Henry James noted, 'His expression is complicated, troubled; but at least there is an interesting mind in it'.[7] His images are troubling. His androgynous male and female figures may have been an attempt to arrive at a form of genetic perfection, akin to an angel, but for some their asexuality is disturbing. He was certainly influenced by the ideals of Botticelli and Michelangelo.[8] Although physically perfect, his knights in shining armour and damsels in distress seem to suffer from 'ennui', a sort of bored indifference, even when faced with the immediate plight of being eaten by a sea monster. On occasions Burne-Jones' view is fatalistic, born out of his own obsession with the 'hand of fate'. He constantly explored grand themes, the sacred and profane, love and loss, sacrifice and reward, good and evil, order and chaos, all the core subjects of myths from the earliest times of human history. At a time when technical reason and scientific investigation called into question the mystical and the spiritual, Burne-Jones transports us into a primordial universe where man faces his destiny, the cycle of life and death. The barren landscapes of *The Perseus Series* do not distract from the significant action, the eternal struggle of good and evil. Only the final panel, the *Baleful Head* presents a lush Garden of Eden, in which our hero is triumphant and duly rewarded.

Burne-Jones' images can be likened to a mirror or a lens through which we peer into an alternative world. Like Lewis Carroll he takes us through the looking glass.[9] It seems that we are happy to accept this world in which the impossible can happen, a world inhabited with monsters, creatures that are half-human and half-beast, gods and goddesses and heroes and heroines. Burne-Jones uses a visual language that 'draws on image, metaphor and narrative in such a way that it evokes ideas, feelings and intuitions in an encompassing way'.[10] Through this language Burne-Jones gives us insight into a world of darkness and light, corruption and renewal. He allows us to confront our worst fears and yet he always gives us hope. He offers us something high to aim for, goals that can be achieved but only through diligence and hard work, a kind of dogged determination to rise above the mundane and ordinary, the perpetual rush of life, to the transcendental.

In Burne-Jones' world spiritual values are paramount. This was his personal response to the debasement of art, as paintings and sculptures were now just another commodity to be bought and sold and generally exploited. Art was all too often purchased for the wrong reasons, for social enhancement or as a financial investment. For many art was a distraction, as patronage and collecting gave the leisured or 'unoccupied classes' something to do. For those with aspirations, cultivating an artistic persona promised social mobility. However, at all levels of society, art was seen to be educationally enriching. As a force for good, with the power to civilise, art assumed a moral dimension.[11] Through his relationship with John Ruskin and William Morris, Burne-Jones was coupled with this notion of art, or beauty, as a force for good, 'the love of which empowers us to do and be good'.[12] Like Morris, Burne-Jones believed that an 'instinct for beauty ... is inborn in every complete man' and therefore, art was a 'positive necessity of life'.[13] Conversely a lack of beauty would dehumanise and brutalise mankind. Burne-Jones professed not to mind that his works appeared next to advertisements for toothpaste, as long as the public had access to beauty.

Yet the artist's own attitude to the moral purpose of art was far from certain. The viewer's response to his complex, even contradictory, images was to be entirely personal. Burne-Jones was not concerned with allegory, something universally understood and devoid of all mystery but, as he tells us himself, with 'types, symbols, suggestions'.[14] The Burne-Jones type is instantaneously recognisable; whether male or female both shared 'the same type of character, expression, and face ... They are all the same person, or of the same family, with the same prominent chin, the same large sickly sad eyes, hollow cheeks, and full lips'.[15] For Burne-Jones, there were only two types of women, those who take the strength out of a man and those who put it back. His innocent maidens are thin, waif-like, with pale complexions, large 'soulful' eyes and mournful expressions. They have an abundance of hair but none of the sensuality of Dante Gabriel Rossetti's Venetian-style temptresses. Gliding in their diaphanous white dresses, his girls have an asexual romanticism that renders them untouchable for they are not of this world. He fashioned a girl who was 'aristocratic in soul or spirit', a commonwealth of beauty not based on social class or blood

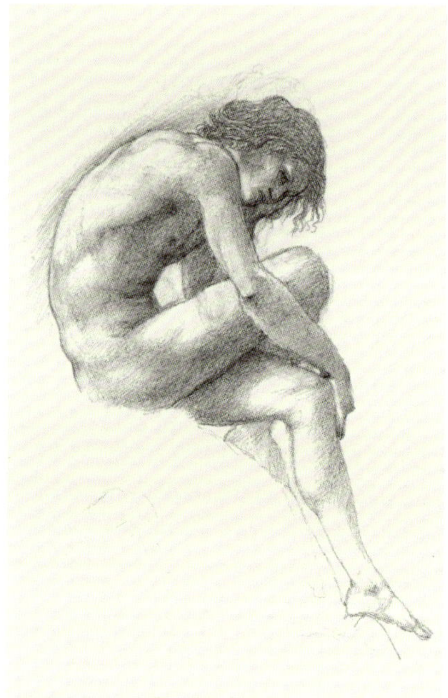

FIG. 2
Study of Perseus for 'The Call of Perseus',
*c.*1877, pencil on paper
© Tate, London 2018

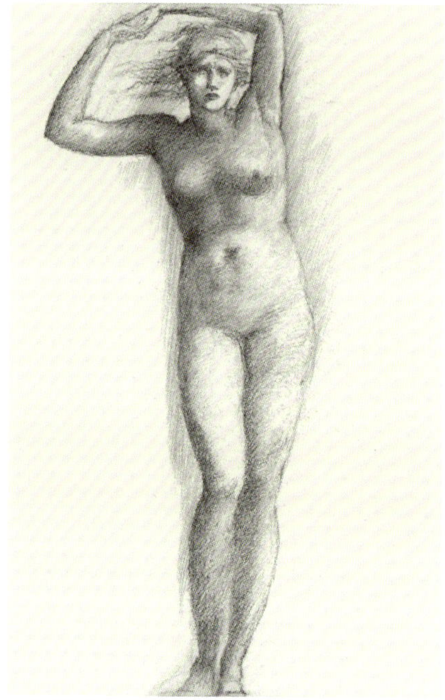

FIG. 3
Study of Medusa for 'The Finding of Medusa',
*c.*1877, pencil on paper
© Tate, London 2018

lineage but on an intuitive response to art and beauty.[16] A love of art was to be the great social leveller, overcoming accidents of birth, fortune or education. As Morris declared, a love of art was universal and was to be 'shared by gentle and simple, learned and unlearned, and be as a language that all can understand'.[17] Burne-Jones' language is challenging, as he communicates with us 'soul to soul'.[18] He credits us with his own rarefied sensibilities. Through beauty we all can attain spiritual transfiguration, can be lifted out of ourselves to a higher plane. However, the notion of an aesthetic elite, 'an aristocracy of mind or spirit dwelling among the teeming masses of the modern age', was also implicit within this notion, as was recognised by Oscar Wilde.[19]

However, the Burne-Jones type did not command universal appeal. The artist was condemned for his lifeless poses, vacant expressions and melancholia: 'the lugubriousity with which E. Burne-Jones clouds every countenance, even that of Love and the Goddess Venus, he will lift someday when his philosophy is riper and healthier – when he has discovered that all mankind, especially womankind, do not walk about the world like hired mutes at a funeral'.[20] The quest for the unattainable led to self-absorption, which in turn resulted in bodily decline and melancholia. In his operetta *Patience* (1881), the famous satire on hyper-aesthesia, W.S. Gilbert prosaically concluded this sickness was caused by unrequited love. As popularised on the stage and in satiric cartoons by George du Maurier and Edward Linley Sambourne, the *High Art Maiden* was simply love-sick. The French art critic Octave Mirbeau found the Burne-Jones type easy prey:

> *... a soul is only a flake, with, here and there, a lily, an iris and a poppy ... Sometimes she holds a lyre in her hand, or a frond ... and her eyes are drawn and blackened ... When people would explain Burne-Jones to me long ago, they would say: 'Please note the hematoma around the eyes; it*

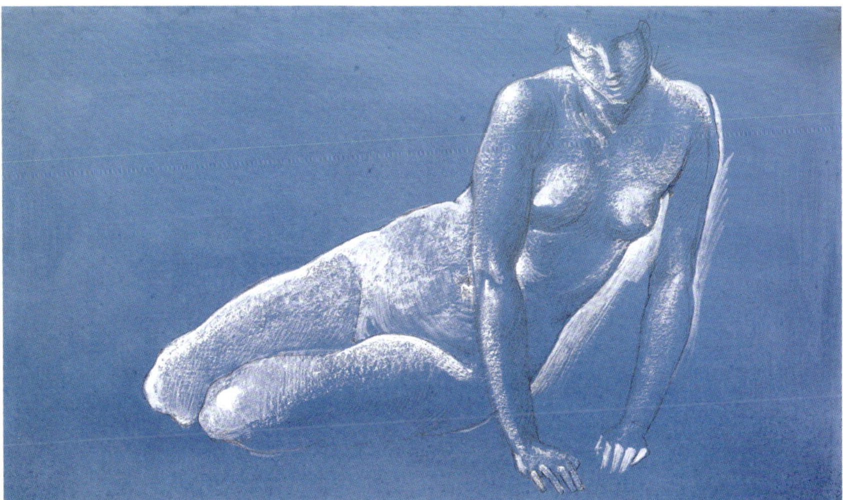

FIG. 4

Sketchbook – Nude Study of Medusa for 'The Death of Medusa I', 1875–79, white bodycolour with white chalk over pencil, on blue watercolour paper *is unique in art. One cannot tell whether it is occasioned by self-abuse or lesbian practices, by natural love or by tuberculosis … That is the key to everything'.*[21]

However, as Henry James noted Burne-Jones was:

… not a votary of the actual … It is beside the mark to say that his young women are sick, for they are neither sick nor well. They live in a different world from ours – a fortunate world in which young ladies may be slim and pale and 'seedy without discredit and (I trust) without discomfort. It is not a question of sickness and health; it is a question of grace, delicacy, tenderness, of the chord of association and memory.[22]

Burne-Jones created a type of beauty that is as recognisable as that of Botticelli or Rossetti. As types his figures were bound to be 'monotonous', his compositions 'conceptions', his subjects 'unreal', the treatment 'artificial' and the intention 'obscure' but, 'If his figures are too much of the same family, no English painter of our day has mastered a single type so completely and made it an image of so many different things'.[23]

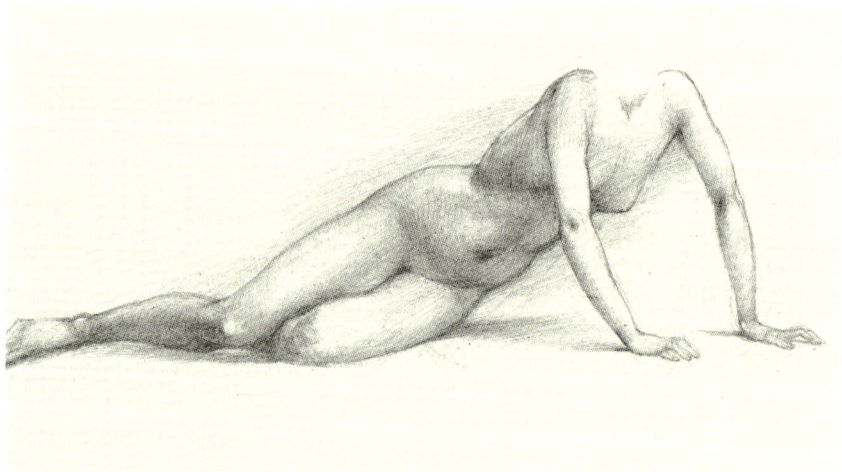

FIG. 5
Study of Medusa for 'The Death of Medusa', c.1877, pencil on paper
© Tate, London 2018

The Perseus Series

The Perseus Legend was commissioned by Arthur James Balfour (1848–1930), created Earl of Balfour in 1922. Alexander Henderson, later 1st Lord Faringdon (1850–1934), would acquire *The Perseus Legend* cartoons, now in Southampton, and the *Legend of the Briar Rose*, which still hangs at Buscot Park, Oxfordshire, the two most important series conceived by Burne-Jones.

Balfour reached the pinnacle of his political career in 1902, when he was elected Prime Minster. However, in the 1890s 'King Arthur', as he was known among his friends, dominated The Souls, a social circle that encompassed both the country's intellectual elite and its most distinguished women, those renowned for their beauty, intelligence or wit. The Souls were drawn from Britain's illustrious families: the Curzons, Wyndhams, Charterises, Tennants, Custs, Windsors and Grenfells. They formally came together in 1889 for a party thrown for George Curzon and again in 1898 to honour Curzon's appointment as Viceroy of India. As Consuelo Marlborough observed they were 'A brilliant company, a select group in which a high degree of intelligence was to be found happily allied to aristocratic birth ... I think there is some justification for the name of "Souls", since many have become immortal'.[24] The Souls looked down on the crude amusements and vulgar ostentation of the 'Marlborough House Set' which centred on Edward, Prince of Wales. As habitués of the Grosvenor Gallery rather than the Royal Academy, The Souls favoured Burne-Jones and George Frederick Watts. Living up to their soubrette they preferred to contemplate visionary, spiritual or poetic subjects rather than banal scenes of everyday life. However, the quest for the transcendental, eschewing all earthly matters, did not bode well for one's finances. Balfour was not good with money. Although his inheritance was reputed to be worth a million pounds, at his death much of this fortune was gone. Injudicious speculations, coupled with neglect of his Scottish estate, left his family in serious debt.[25]

Balfour was the quintessential Soul, the circle's High Priest; he was a 'fixed Sun round which the lesser luminaries revolve. I doubt, indeed, if he were extinguished, whether the society could exist without the clear electric light which they derive from his *spirituelle* nature'.[26] Apparently, his 'charm and intellectual distinction gave the group an aura which transcended social considerations'.[27] While at Trinity College, Cambridge, Balfour acquired an interest in metaphysical speculation. This led him to publish his *Defence of Philosophical Doubt* (1878). This was primarily an attempt to reconcile religion and science. Balfour certainly gained a reputation for being indecisive; allegedly when faced with the double staircase in his London home, 4, Carlton Gardens, he was unable to decide which side to take. Many were fooled by Balfour's languid manner and 'air of dilettantish affectation'; his original political soubrette, 'Miss Fanny' was soon superseded by 'Bloody Balfour' when he ruthlessly suppressed agitation in Ireland.[28] By 1891 he was the acknowledged heir apparent to the Conservative leadership.

For Balfour life amongst The Souls was an escape from the political arena. He could relax, indulging in idle or amusing chatter. Moreover, The Souls were 'interested in really interesting things' and were even 'alive to the claims of Art'.[29] They blended politics with fashion and fashion with philanthropy; their 'sacrifice to Beauty, Truth and Goodness' was enacted before a 'background of West-end dinner parties and great country-houses'.[30] Yet this warm sociability masked Balfour's profound pessimism. Did Balfour find an echo of his own doubts in the paintings of Burne-Jones? Writing in *The Foundation of Belief*, he revealed an unshakable conviction that man was unimportant in a perishable universe; 'Man will go down into the pit and all his thoughts will perish'.[31] In his *Chapters in Autobiography*, Balfour succeeds in maintaining his mask, cloaking his emotional turmoil with a carefully constructed urbane facade. Despite the close circle that surrounded him with affection, he remained aloof; 'no misfortune, no bereavement, could have broken him, for he was solitary at heart'.[32] At the root of this emotional detachment laid May Lyttelton whom he had loved and lost; she died in March 1875. Balfour maintained they were engaged, even placing his mother's ring in her coffin. Throughout his life Balfour used May as a means of retreat from romantic liaisons; he remained a bachelor. Nevertheless, there was one amorous relationship that did sustain him; Mary Wyndham, who married Hugo, Lord Elcho, remained his confidant for fifty years. Wilfred Blunt, himself a notorious philanderer, concluded 'their love should be within certain limits – a little more than friendship, a little less than love'.[33]

In 1875, shortly after May's death, looking for a means of distracting Balfour at this difficult time, Blanche, Lady Airlie took him to meet Burne-

Jones in his studio. For a man who would have preferred a life of undisturbed philosophical speculation, Burne-Jones must have seemed a kindred spirit; he 'at once fell prey both to the man and his art'.[34] A major commission ensued; to decorate the walls of the music-room at Carlton Gardens, the town house Balfour had purchased in 1871, with a 'series of pictures characteristic of his art':[35]

> *It so happened that the principal drawing-room was, as London drawing-rooms go, long and well lit, and the happy thought occurred to me to ask my new friend to design for it a series of pictures characteristic of his art … The subject I left entirely to him. The choice of the Perseus Legend was therefore not mine, but I have never regretted it.*[36]

A series of panel paintings was proposed illustrating the Greek legend of Perseus: 'I have just had a commission I shall like for a young man named Balfour … he wants pictures to go round a room, some story or another which will be very pleasant work – he is very delightful and amicable and so young it is painful'.[37] Balfour was only twenty-six.

Burne-Jones had already completed *The St George Series* (1865–67) for the watercolour artist Miles Birket Foster. Seven canvases were hung in the dining room of his country house, The Hill, Witley, Surrey. The paintings took two years to complete, with the help of Burne-Jones' studio assistant Charles Fairfax Murray. The subject may have been inspired by William Morris' *The Earthly Paradise*, which was certainly the source for the *Cupid and Psyche* panels begun in 1872 for George Howard's town house, 1 Palace Green, Kensington. Twelve panels were designed for the dining room; having enthusiastically undertaken the project, filling two sketch books and starting on the panels, Burne-Jones ceded its completion to Walter Crane. The panels were finally installed in 1881. Balfour patiently endured a long wait for his commissioned works; indeed the series was never completed. Burne-Jones wryly observed that the paintings grew 'as slowly as granite hills'.[38] According to the artist's son Philip, Balfour never tried 'in any way to haste him in the matter which he understood did not admit of haste, and my father fully realised and appreciated his considerate conduct'.[39] However, he did on one occasion forestall completion by objecting to the severed head of the Gorgon, in *The Death of Medusa II*. During his long wait, Balfour consoled himself by buying other

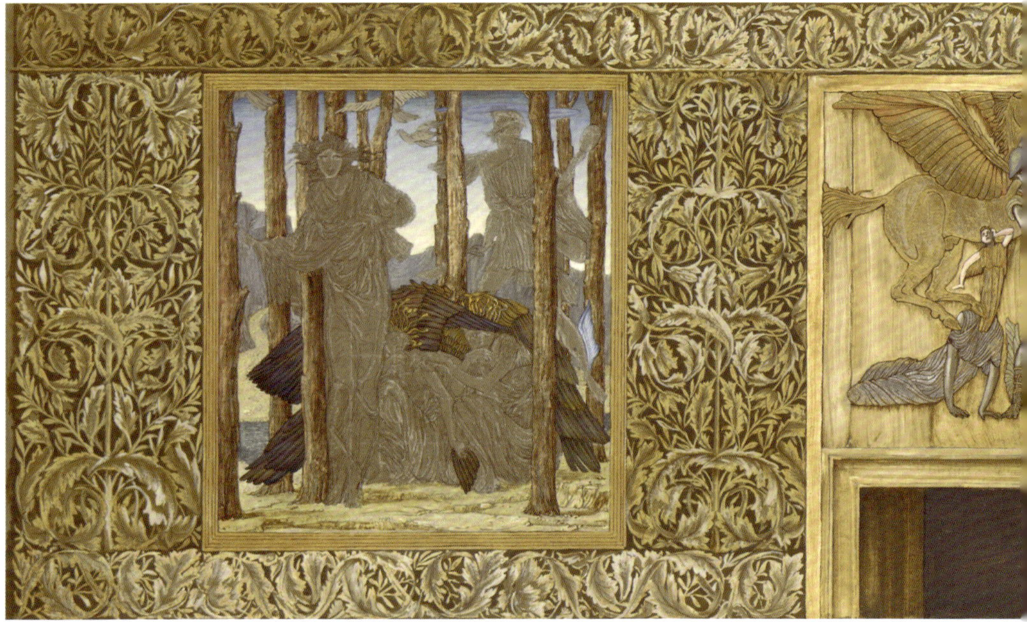

FIG. 6

Designs for *The Perseus Series: The Finding of Medusa; The Death of Medusa (The Birth of Pegasus and Chyrsaor); Perseus Pursued by the Gorgons*, 1875–76, gouache, gold paint and ink on paper

© Tate, London 2018

paintings, notably *The Wheel of Fortune* (1875–83). He may have seen this work in progress on that first, fateful, visit to Burne-Jones' studio.

Burne-Jones turned to Morris's 'The Doom of King Acrisius' in the *Earthly Paradise* for his narrative. The Perseus legend gave Burne-Jones the opportunity to depict his most favoured themes, the conquest of good over evil and the triumph of beauty, encapsulated in a narrative sequence. He devised a sequence of ten subjects, mapped out over three large designs: 1. *The Call of Perseus; Perseus and the Graiae; Perseus and the Nereids*; 2. *The Finding of Medusa; The Death of Medusa (The Birth of Pegasus and Chrysaor); Perseus Pursued by the Gorgons* (fig. 6); and 3. *Atlas Turned to Stone; The Rock of Doom and The Doom Fulfilled; The Court of Phineas; The Baleful Head*.

These indicated the position of each work in the sequence and how they were to be integrated into a unified work of art. They were to be framed

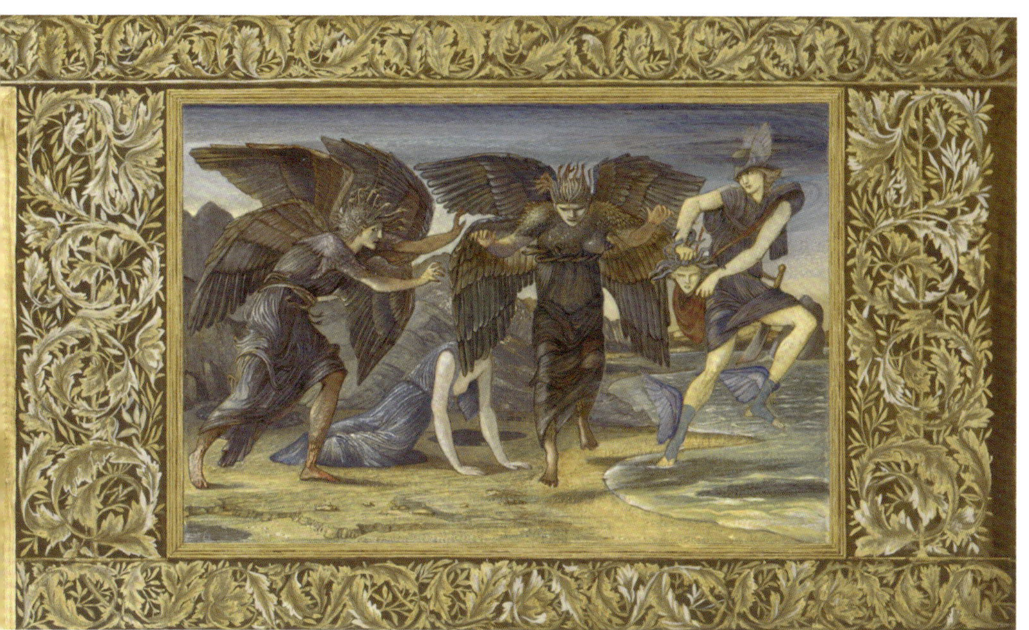

with plasterwork, an acanthus design by Morris. On 27 March 1875 Burne-Jones visited Carlton Gardens to survey the site intended for his paintings.[40] In his report, which Balfour kept in his letterbook, Burne-Jones informed his client that as the lighting in the music room was too harsh all the windows needed to be re-glazed.[41] Light English oak panelling would have to be installed from the floor to a height of six and a half feet. This would be surmounted by the paintings, hung in a band 'resembling the procession by Mantegna at Hampton Court'. He also recommended candlelight to create a sympathetic ambience for the paintings. He decreed the 'whole room should be in harmony and the whole should look as if nothing was an afterthought but all had naturally grown together'. Burne-Jones admitted the room would not 'go' with the rest of the well appointed house. But 'what can one do in these days, with the inheritance of a hundred years of ugliness and dreariness before us, but clear a little space

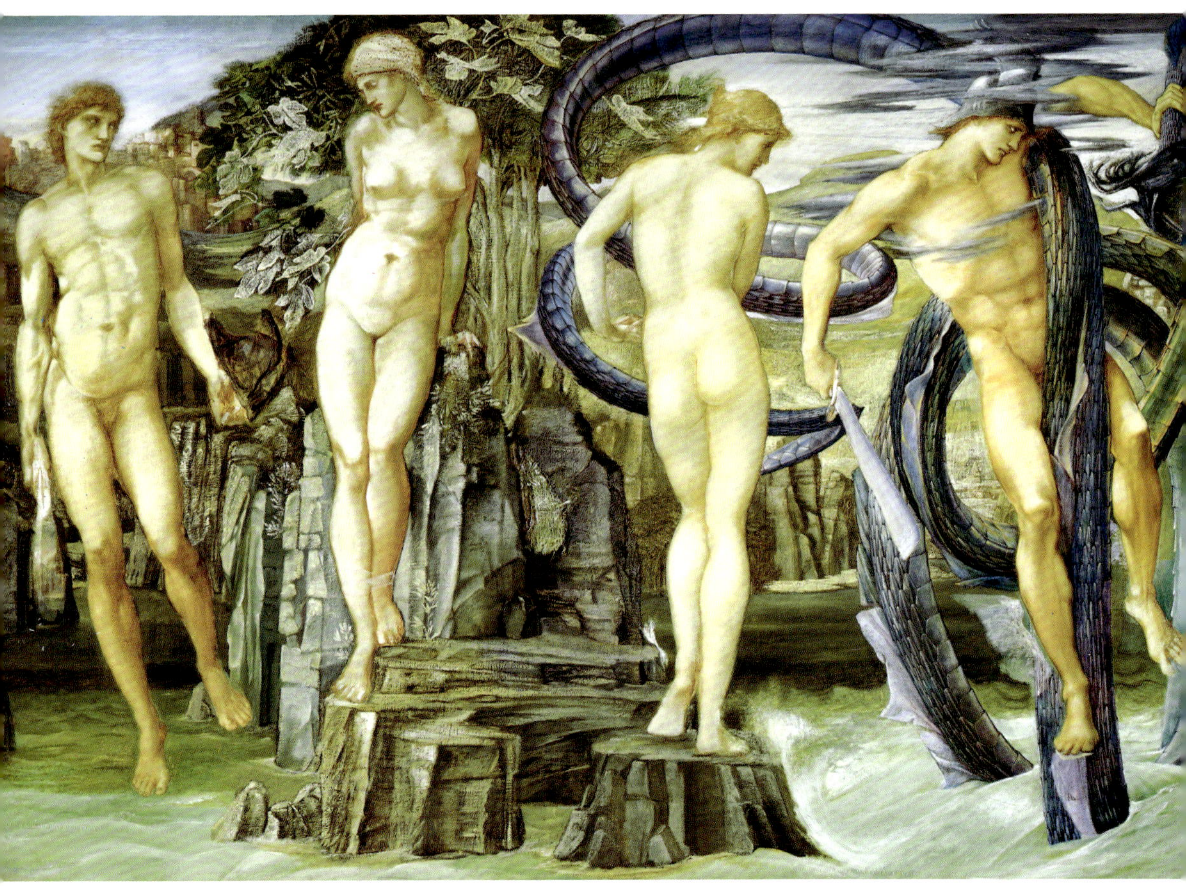

FIG. 7
Perseus and Andromeda, 1876, oil on canvas

© Art Gallery of South Australia, Adelaide, Australia (Elder Bequest Fund)/Bridgeman Images as a sort of testimony that that we don't like it although we have to bear it'.[42] Clearly this dimly lit room, imbued with a mystical atmosphere verging on the sacred, was meant to offer respite from the modern world and all its impositions. However, this Palace of Art came at a price; Burne-Jones estimated £3,800 for the six canvases alone ('2 longer one £800 each; 3 middle size 600 each; 1 smaller 400').

Balfour approved the sketches, paying £500 on account, and put the expensive alterations in hand. Prophetically, Burne-Jones assured him that 'even if the pictures had to wait and if they were never added the room would still look beautiful'.[43]

As the project evolved, Burne-Jones simplified the narrative concentrating on the central episodes, the quest for the Gorgon Medusa and the rescue of Andromeda. He condensed each design into a single action, although *The Call of Perseus* still uses a traditional pictorial device simultaneously depicting two incidents. Hence Perseus and Athena appear twice in the same continuous landscape. Originally *The Rock of Doom* and *The Doom Fulfilled* were conceived as one panel (fig. 7). Although split, we are still treated to a mirror image of Andromeda, seen from front and behind. Four of the subjects, those above the chimneypiece and the doors, were to be executed as golden gesso panels carved in relief and painted. *Perseus and the Graiae*, the first gesso panel, was placed in the centre of the first wall. Serving as a focal point it carries an inscription explaining the entire story in a Latin text provided by the classical scholar Richard Jebb. Burne-Jones tested this new concept exhibiting *Perseus and the Graiae* (fig. 8) at the Grosvenor Gallery, London, in 1878.[44] Crossing the boundary between sculpture and painting it was not well received: seen in isolation both critics and the public were baffled as they could not understand its purpose. Similarly few appreciated his later attempt to erase the boundary between fine and decorative art by attaching thin sheets of metal to Perseus' armour.[45]

Although Burne-Jones abandoned the remaining gesso panels, *The Death of Medusa (The Birth of Pegasus and Chrysaor)*, to be situated over a doorway, suggests how effective the combination of gilding and low-relief modelling would have been.[46] If the scheme had been completed, the effect would have recalled an Italian Renaissance palazzo interior of the type depicted in Domenico *Ghirlandaio's Birth of Mary* in Santa Maria Novella, Florence (1486–90). This gives us an idea of Burne-Jones's aspirations;

such a scheme, integrating paintings and decor, creating a 'total art work', would finally be realised with the installation of the *Briar Rose* series at Buscot Park in 1895.

His imagination fired by the new subject Burne-Jones took himself off to the British Museum in search of Greek Attic vases that depicted the legend; he looked up 'all the most ancient ways of pourtraying [*sic*] Medusa, and they are few but very interesting, and I know much more about it than I did'.[47] As was his way, numerous preparatory drawings were made. One sketchbook dated July 1875 contains several related studies (figs 9–10).[48]

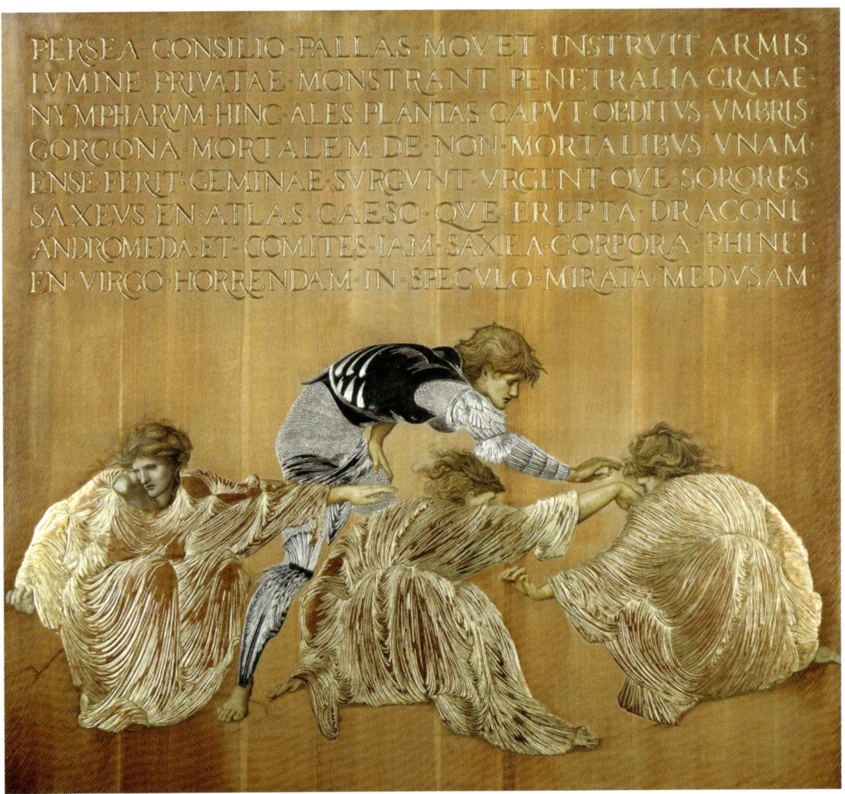

FIG. 8

Perseus and the Graiae, 1877,
oil, bronze and silver leaf on carved gesso on an oak panel overpainted with gold

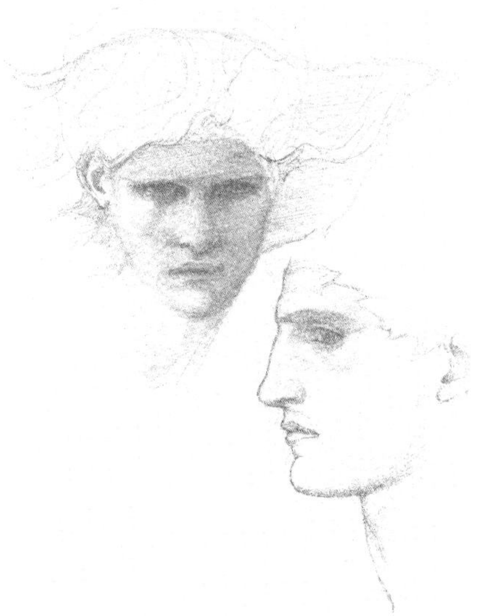

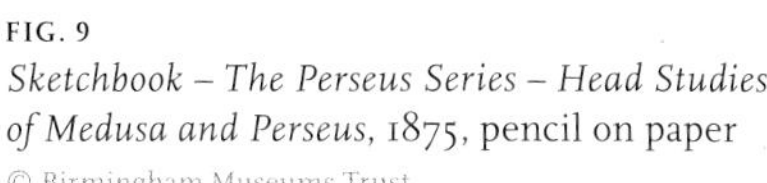

FIG. 9

Sketchbook – The Perseus Series – Head Studies of Medusa and Perseus, 1875, pencil on paper

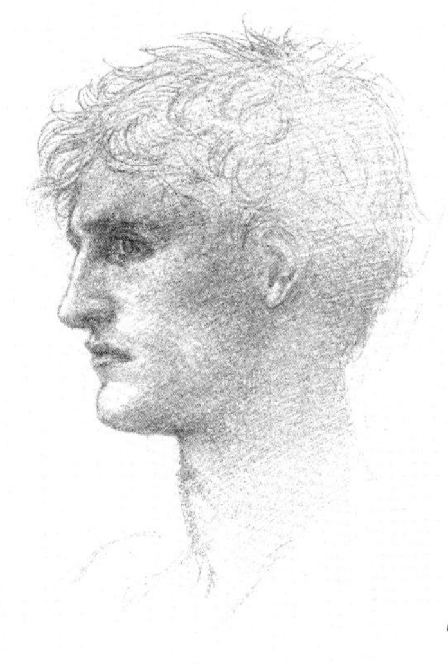

FIG. 10

Sketchbook – Study for the Head of Perseus, 1875, pencil on paper

Many of the surviving drawings, a host of male and female nude studies and draped figures, and alternative monsters, a medley of scales and fins, gnashing teeth and fangs or forked tongues, date from 1875 to 1877. His mental picture also needed to be visualised in three dimensions. He took a week to make a clay model of Perseus; to better gauge the effect he wound a snaky monster round the figure.[49] He told Philip, 'All evening your Mama and I have been shaping a cap for Perseus, and a hosen for him and a sword'; Georgiana recalled 'other strange inventions and substitutions for unattainable realities ... the necessary instruments for his work'.[50]

As Burne-Jones worked on *The Perseus Series* for over twenty years he used many different models. His favoured professional models numbered Augusta Jones (later Johnson), Bessie Keen and Antonia Caiva. Deemed the finest of his nude models, Caiva 'was like Eve and Semiramis but if she had a mind at all, which I always doubted, it had no ideas. She had splendour and solemnity: her glory lasted nearly ten years'.[51] However, in *The Golden Stairs* (1880, Tate) Burne-Jones grafted portraits, likenesses of girls in the

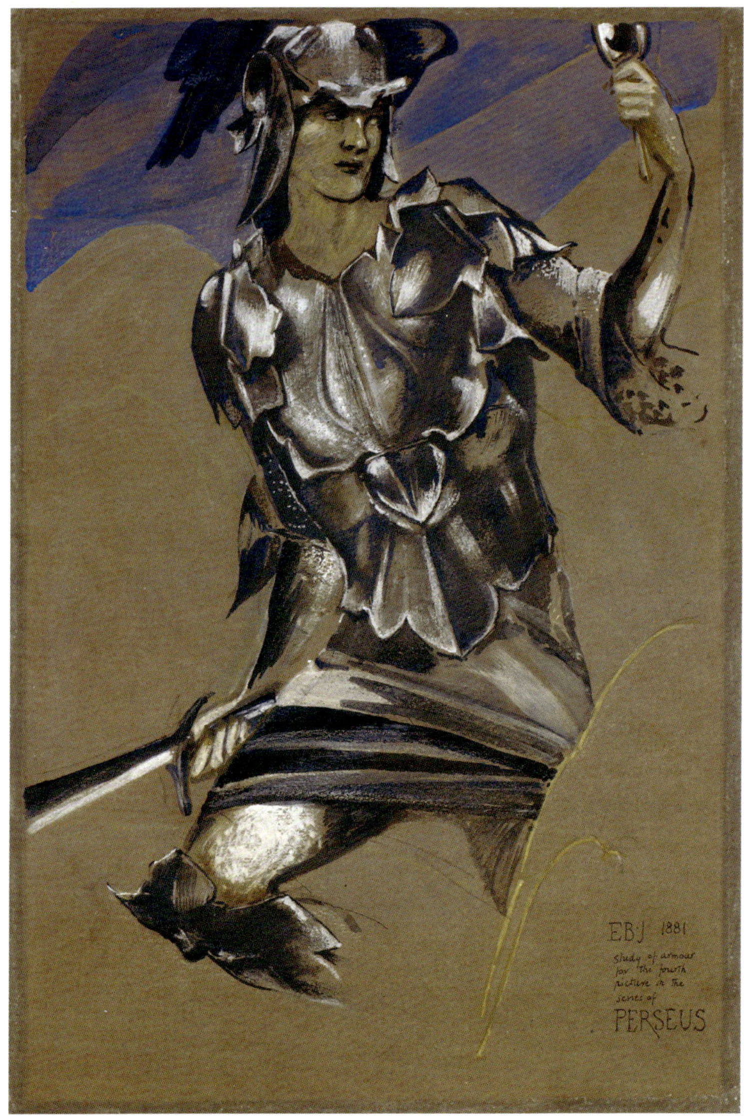

FIG. 11

The Perseus Series – Study of Perseus in Armour for 'The Finding of Medusa', 1881,
watercolour, bodycolour, silver medium and chalk on brown/grey paper

© Birmingham Museums Trust

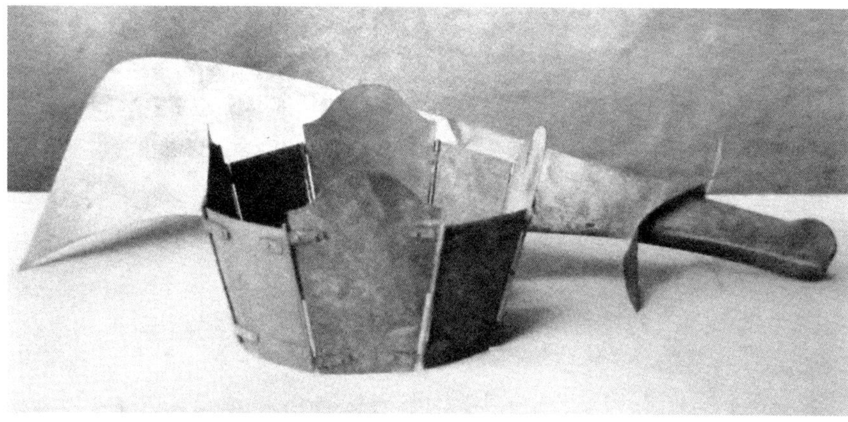

FIG. 12

Model of crown and sword

from 'Notes on Some Unfinished Works of Sir Edward Burne-Jones, Bt., by His Son' by Philip Burne-Jones,
Magazine of Art, vol. 24, 1900, p. 162

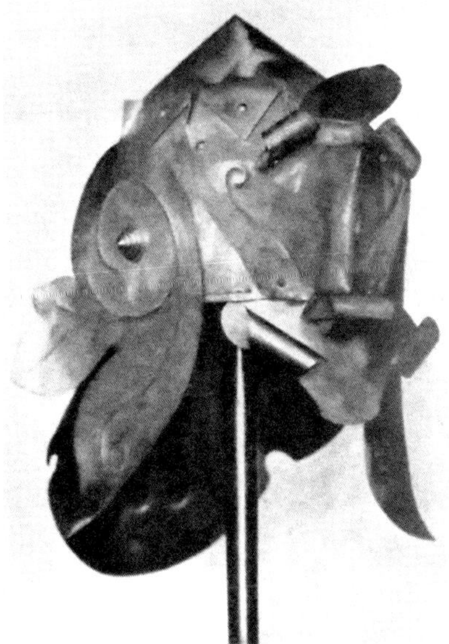

FIG. 13

Model of helmet for Perseus

from *The Decorative Art of Sir Edward Burne-Jones*
(extra number of the *Art Journal*) by Aymer Vallance, 1900,
p. 31, fig. 46

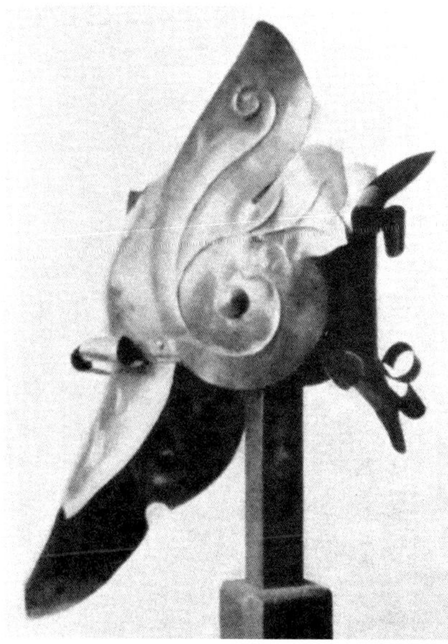

FIG. 14

Model for helmet of Perseus

from 'Notes on Some Unfinished Works of Sir Edward
Burne-Jones, Bt., by His Son', by Philip Burne-Jones,
Magazine of Art, vol. 24, 1900, p. 161

artist's family or circle, onto the body of Caiva. For this painting, he asked his friend George Howard to suggest 'a nice innocent damsel or two' to fill up 'the staircase picture'.[52] Frances Graham (1854–1940), the daughter of Burne-Jones' staunch patron William Graham, is seen moving out of the picture lower left, holding cymbals, while behind stands her close friend Mary Gladstone, the daughter of William Gladstone.[53] Ironically Burne-Jones' attempt to render true likenesses was lost on most critics who concluded the faces were taken from the same model. Indeed it is very difficult to distinguish specific models for his works. Even when he attempted portraits, 'some imperative instinct of selection deflected his hand from what he saw with his eyes to the image of his inner vision'.[54] He admitted, 'I do not easily get portraiture – and the perpetual hunt to find in a face what I like and leave out what mislikes me, is a bad school of it'.[55]

His search for 'a nice innocent damsel' resulted in many drawings, which he returned to for subsequent projects.[56] Frances Graham appears in *Perseus and the Sea Nymphs*. Frances came into Burne-Jones's life at a critical moment; she was eighteen, he forty. His affair with the tempestuous Maria Zambaco (1843–1914), which came close to destroying his marriage, had burnt itself out and he was left a wiser but sadder man. The young Frances detected his loneliness; 'he was not very happy'.[57] Their friendship blossomed into a sentimental, platonic, love that sustained him for the rest of his life.[58] 'Many a patient design went to adorning Frances' ways,' wrote Burne-Jones, 'Sirens for her girdle, Heavens and Paradises for her prayer-books, Virtues and Vices for her necklace-boxes – ah! The folly of me from the beginning.'[59] Her marriage to Sir John 'Jack' Horner in 1883 caused him heart-ache but their friendship remained of vital importance to him. During the 1880s she became a leading light of The Souls. A foil to Balfour, Lady Paget called Frances the 'High Priestess' of the set, referencing her close relationship with Burne-Jones who was deemed the arbiter of their taste.[60] Perhaps Burne-Jones found solace by gazing at Frances' beautiful face in *Perseus and the Sea Nymphs* as it hung on his studio wall.

It is tempting to speculate Burne-Jones cast Maria Zambaco as Medusa, as a way of exorcising her ghost; she features in the *Beguiling of Merlin* (1872–77, Lady Lever Art Gallery) with Medusa-like snakes in her hair. But it is said Margaret Benson provided her features, a face he found by chance.[61] From Rossetti, Burne-Jones acquired the habit of pursing a face seen in the street, the elusive *passante* (passer-by) of poet Charles

Baudelaire, 'leading to an intense relationship between artist and model, product itself of the great city with its countless dreamers and strugglers through the fog'.[62] According to Fitzgerald, 'in this matter Burne-Jones was exacting. His poesias depended on the relationship between the story, the face and the experience it reflected'.[63] Such a chance encounter occurred in 1877 at a rehearsal of Wagner at the Albert Hall. Burne-Jones spotted a 'young girl whose head was of a type that he knew would be helpful to him in his Perseus pictures'.[64] An introduction was procured, her mother admitting 'she has often been called my Burne-Jones daughter'. The Miss Benson in question was Margaret Benson, later Mrs Drummond; 'many were the studies he made of her'.[65] Burne-Jones came to know many of the Benson clan. Her brother W.A.S. Benson apparently supplied the head of 'Pygmalion'.[66] A talented metal-worker, Benson designed and made a crown for 'King Cophetua' (*King Cophetua and the Beggar Maid*, 1884, Tate). He also lent a hand with Perseus' armour; 'Endless studies of armour were made ... Sir Coutts Lindsay had a fine collection of old armour from which Edward made drawings, and in addition to this, with the help of Mr Benson, he designed many pieces himself, expressly in order to lift them out of association with any historical time'.[67]

While Benson could have modelled for Perseus, during the 1870s Burne-Jones favoured Italian models Alessandro di Marco, Angelo Colarossi and Gaetano Meo. Alessandro di Marco first modelled for Frederic Leighton as a small child; he appears in *Cimabue's Celebrated Madonna* (1855, Royal Collection, on long-term loan to the National Gallery, London). By the late 1860s he was modelling in London for Leighton, William Blake Richmond, Edward Poynter, Alphonse Legros, Dante Gabriel Rossetti, and the photographer Julia Margaret Cameron. Richmond described him as 'a fellow so graceful and of such a colour, a kind of bronze gold, having a skin of so fine a texture that the movement of every muscle was not disguised, not a film of fat disfigured his shapely limbs. Only a peasant, people say! Yes – but of a race of Kings – so noble he looked.'[68] Alessandro is believed to have sat for *The Beguiling of Merlin* of 1872–77 (Lady Lever Art Gallery, Port Sunlight) and the watercolour version of *Love Among the Ruins* (Christie's, London, 11 July 2013, lot 3).[69] However, according to Martin Harrison and Bill Walters, the model for Perseus was a gypsy named Smith.[70]

Full-scale cartoons in watercolour and bodycolour were begun in 1877 and completed in 1885. According to Philip Burne-Jones it was his father's custom to 'draw out upon brown paper, the same size as the intended canvas, an elaborate scheme in colour for the picture he was about to paint. This preliminary design or cartoon was usually drawn in pastel or watercolour, often a mixture of the two'.[71] Some of the Perseus cartoons are drawn on brown paper. Their five foot dimensions would have required two or three conjoined pieces, as the maximum sized sheet available was 53 inches.[72] In the unfinished *Death of Medusa II* large areas of dark brown paper are visible, squared up with white chalk in preparation for painting. It is known that Burne-Jones purchased three strainers with 'linen and brown paper', whose dimensions exactly match those of the first three Perseus cartoons, during 1877.[73]

Only four of the panels were painted in oils; these are all now in the Staatsgalerie Stuttgart, along with two unfinished canvases and two duplicate cartoons. *The Baleful Head* was shown at the Grosvenor Gallery in 1887; the *Punch* cartoonist Harry Furniss re-imagined this as 'The Ogress at the Stores' with 'Nice fresh heads today, Ma'am!' (fig. 16).[74] Although *Punch* mocked the pretensions of contemporary art, the magazine's extensive coverage guaranteed Burne-Jones' celebrity status. *The Rock of Doom* and *The Doom Fulfilled* were exhibited, alongside *Danae (The Tower of Brass)*, at the New Gallery in May 1888.[75] Opened in direct opposition to the Grosvenor Gallery, Furniss made fun of this new venture. In his cartoon Burne-Jones is shown with a long shaggy beard and bald pate, his nose distinctly red and holding a glass of stout. Evidently during the opening everybody got very hot but no refreshments could be procured as the proprietors had been unable to secure a licence. In the background Andromeda from *The Doom Fulfilled* can be seen cooling down under a shower provided by Perseus. Exclaiming, 'Drat these new pipes!', Perseus is grappling with the monster now transformed into a water pipe. Standing opposite, cowering behind a column, Andromeda from *The Rock of Doom*, appears to be playing hide and seek (fig. 15).

Burne-Jones' health broke under the strain of completing these monumental works. Unable to attend the private view, apparently he 'fled to Rottingdean but the quality of the pictures themselves was not in doubt'.[76] Writing in the *Academy*, Cosmo Monkhouse mused the paintings could be admired merely for their decorative effect, as simply arrangements of form and colour, but 'the artist will not allow us to do this. He appeals to our emotions. The pictures are intended to be a power to the soul as well as a

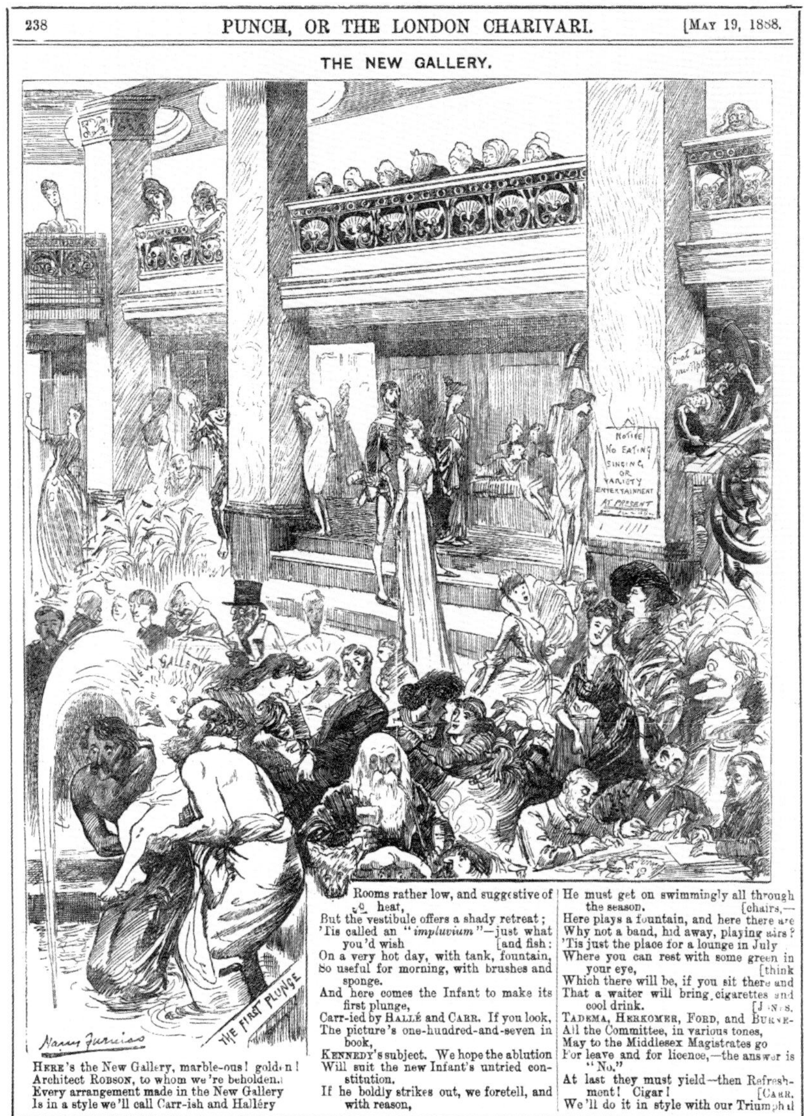

Here's the New Gallery, marble-ous! golden!
Architect Robson, to whom we're beholden.
Every arrangement made in the New Gallery
Is in a style we'll call Carr-ish and Halléry

Rooms rather low, and suggestive of heat,
But the vestibule offers a shady retreat;
'Tis called an "*impluvium*"—just what you'd wish
On a very hot day, with tank, fountain, [and fish:
So useful for morning, with brushes and sponge.
And here comes the Infant to make its first plunge,
Carr-ied by Hallé and Carr. If you look,
The picture's one-hundred-and-seven in book,
Kennedy's subject. We hope the ablution
Will suit the new Infant's untried constitution.
If he boldly strikes out, we foretell, and with reason,

He must get on swimmingly all through the season.
Here plays a fountain, and here there are [chairs,—
Why not a band, hid away, playing airs?
'Tis just the place for a lounge in July
Where you can rest with some green in your eye, [think
Which there will be, if you sit there and
That a waiter will bring cigarettes and cool drink. [Jones.
Tadema, Herkomer, Ford, and Burne-
All the Committee, in various tones,
May to the Middlesex Magistrates go
For leave and for licence,—the answer is "No."
At last they must yield—then Refreshment! Cigar! [Carr.
We'll do it in style with our Triumphal

FIG. 15

'The New Gallery' by Harry Furniss

from *Punch*, vol. 104, 19 May 1888, p. 238

pleasure to the eyes'.[77] M.M. Spielmann also admired their beauty; 'these works, three of a long series, possess that rare decorative beauty of which Mr Burne-Jones alone has the secret'.[78]

It was not until the artist's death that Balfour finally took possession of his paintings. They were briefly displayed at Carlton Gardens before being installed in the state dining room of 10 Downing Street during Balfour's premiership (1902–06). The newly elected Unionist M.P. Willie Bridgeman perceived a synergy between the paintings and their owner; 'The room was full of very excellent Burne-Jones pictures, whose anaemic and unmanly forms seemed to give the meeting a nerveless and flabby character, and were to me painfully symbolic of their owner'.[79] Many contemporary commentators found Burne-Jones' treatment dispassionate and lacking in human interest which, as luck would have it, reflected the owner's heartless reputation. The artist never relinquished the cartoons. They were framed and displayed in his garden studio, where they were

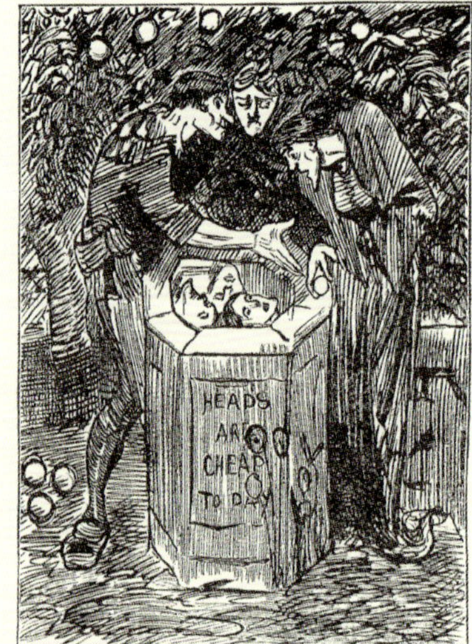

No. 75. The Ogress at the Stores. "Nice fresh Heads to-day, Ma'am!"

FIG. 16
'The Ogress at the Stores' by Harry Furniss
from *Punch*, vol. 102, 14 May 1887, p. 238

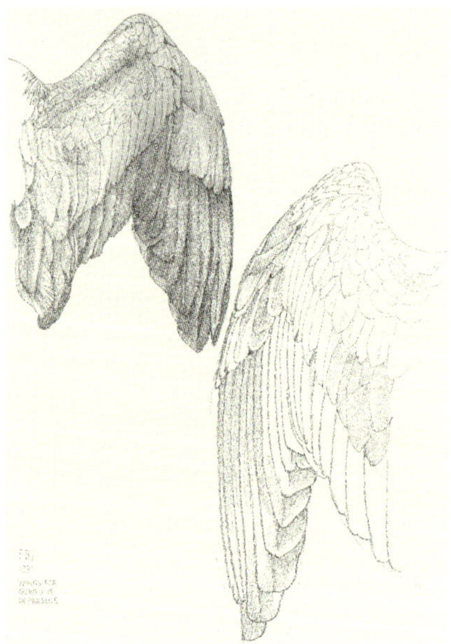

FIG. 17
The Perseus Series – Study of Wings for 'The Death of Medusa', 1881, pencil on paper
© Birmingham Museums Trust

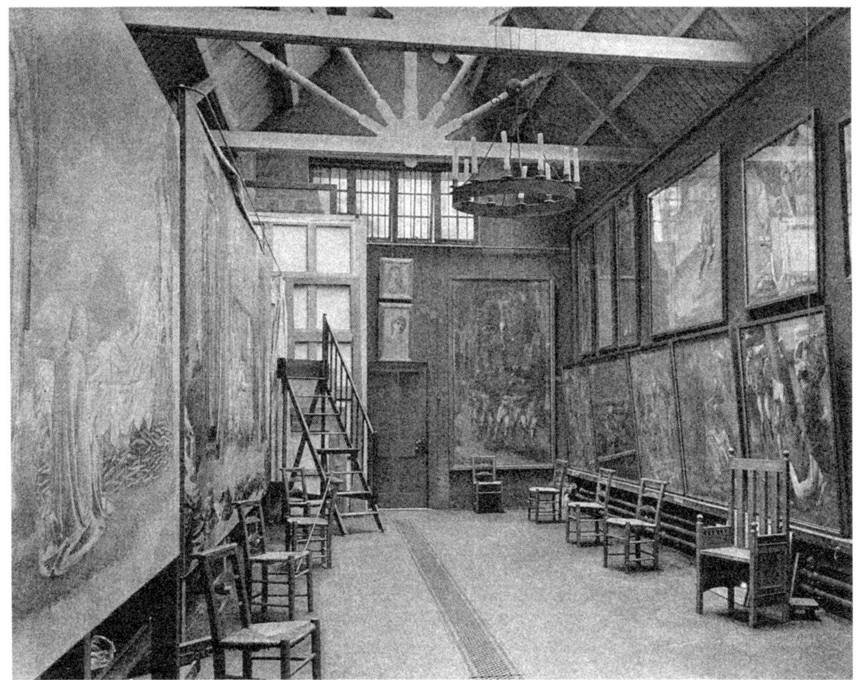

FIG. 18
Edward Burne-Jones's garden studio
from *The Life and Work of Edward Burne-Jones* (Christmas number of the *Art Journal*) by Julia Cartwright, 1894, p. 31, fig. 39

admired by friends and visitors (fig. 18). Graham Robertson claimed they 'far surpassed any of them that ever reached completion'.[80]

A major memorial exhibition of Burne-Jones' work was held at the New Gallery in the winter of 1898 to 1899, the artist having died the previous June. Balfour lent his paintings (*Perseus and the Graiae, The Rock of Doom, The Doom Fulfilled, The Baleful Head*). Simultaneously an *Exhibition of Drawings and Studies* was held at the Burlington Fine Arts Club. Works relating to the Perseus series numbered 'Fine studies of wings lent by the executors' (124, 154); 'Mr Theobald's two heads of Perseus' (61); 'Mr Fairfax Murray's splendid drawing of Perseus and the Monster' (106); and 'the finest of all the artist's pencil drawings of the nude, Mr Reece's Andromeda' (127). The finished drawings of the whole scheme (116, 117, 118), 'the most important of the many treasures lent by the Executors', illustrated 'most completely the artist's imagination in its full power over both the beautiful and the terrible, as well as his decorative skill'.[81] Significantly, none of the ten full sized cartoons were shown.[82]

Their acquisition by financier Alexander Henderson, later 1st Lord Faringdon (1850–1934), who had already acquired a taste for Burne-Jones, remains unclear. There is no entry for them in Henderson's 'Own Picture Catalogue' of 1894. This gives his Burne-Jones pictures as *Spes* (Dunedin Public Art Gallery) and *Fides* (Vancouver Art Gallery) both large water-colours on panels signed and dated 1871 and 1872 respectively; *The Angels of Creation* six panels (Harvard) painted 1876–77;[83] *Cupid and Psyche* (Hammersmith and Fulham Council), watercolour on canvas, signed 1867.[84] The final catalogue listing is *The Briar Rose* 'with numerous smaller decorative subjects and panels of subsidiary subjects, inserted in the wall framing between the four larger pictures (1876–90)'. By *c.*1902, the innovative firm of Braun et C. Paris, Dornach, and New York, had issued a set of ten carbon prints of the Perseus cartoons with French titles, copyrighted 1902–05, which are credited as belonging to the 'Collection Alexander Henderson ESQ. M.P.'.[85] It should also be noted that Henderson was created a baronet in 1902 and baron in 1916.

Henderson, the second son of a distinguished Greek and Hebrew scholar, George Henderson of Langholm, Dumfries, began his career at Deloittes, a leading firm of accountants. Soon after he joined the stock-broking firm Greenwood & Co. A leading figure in the City, he financed a wide range of industrial and business enterprises particularly railways. He was chairman of the Great Central Railway from 1889 until its re-organisation in 1922. *The Perseus Series* was destined for 52 Princes Gate, Kensington, Henderson's London residence recently acquired from Thomas Eustace Smith, MP.[86] The paintings then moved to Henderson's next London home, 18 Arlington Street, also known as Pomfret Castle, which was demolished after his death in 1934.[87] Henderson purchased Buscot Park, Oxfordshire in 1889, where Burne-Jones' *Legend of the Briar Rose* can still be seen in situ. This series was not commissioned by one of Burne-Jones's long standing patrons. Rather Agnew's of Bond Street paid £15,000 for the paintings.[88] All four were finished by April 1890 being exhibited in the summer to 'ever increasing crowds of delighted visitors'.[89] Purchased by Henderson they were installed in the drawing-room at Buscot Park.[90] While staying with Morris at nearby Kelmscott Manor, Burne-Jones was able to see the paintings in their new setting. Dissatisfied with the hanging he completed ten additional panels, without figures, to create a continuous sequence set in an elaborate gilded framework. Henderson amassed a magnificent collection, ranging from Rembrandt to Botticelli, though it is difficult to gauge its richness as it was dispersed at his death. G.F. Watts, *Choosing* (1864, National Portrait Gallery) and John Everett Millais' *Esther* (1865, private collection) were sold at auction in July 1934. *The Perseus Series* was purchased by Southampton City Art Gallery from his widow Lady Violet Henderson for £3,500.[91]

The Perseus Series cartoons are a unique and treasured part of Southampton City Art Gallery's outstanding collection. Although Balfour never saw the full Perseus series installed in his music room, the cartoons now hang in a room similar to that originally intended. This room stands apart from the rest of the other galleries; rather than pristine white walls it has rich, dark mahogany panels incorporating a large marble fireplace. These fittings, dating to 1913, come from the boardroom of Baring Brothers and Company, merchant bankers, at 8 Bishopsgate, London. In 1975 the bank's headquarters were demolished to make way for new roads and in the spirit of European Architectural Heritage Year, Baring Brothers presented the boardroom fittings to Southampton City Council. The Baring Room was carefully reassembled by a team of highly skilled craftsmen from Vosper Thornycroft, members of the Union of Construction, Allied Trades and Technicians to create a beautiful new setting in the City Art Gallery. This room made an ideal backdrop for *The Perseus Series* and so, in late 1975 the works were installed and have been displayed there ever since.

overleaf
The Baring Room, Southampton City Art Gallery
photograph Joe Low

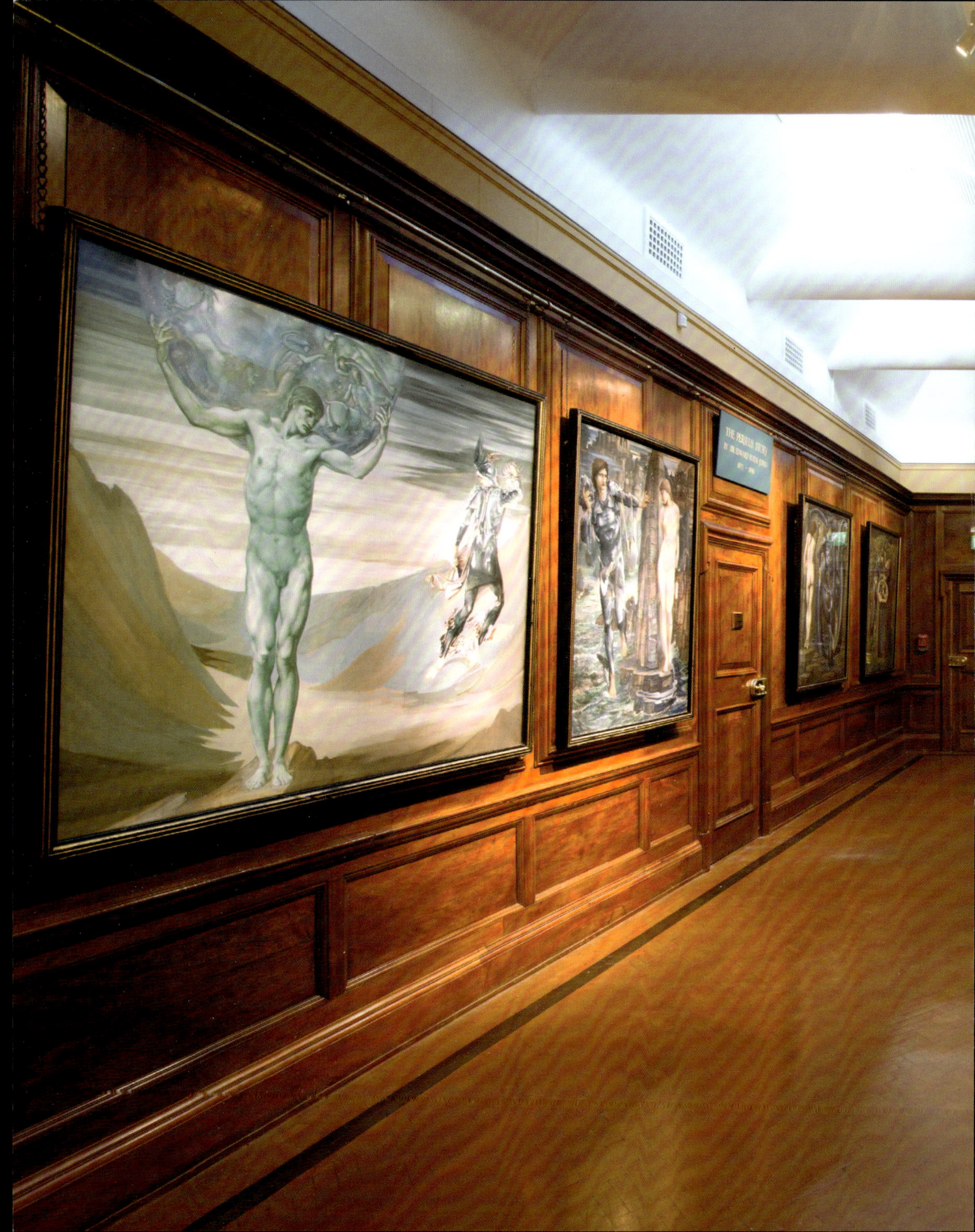

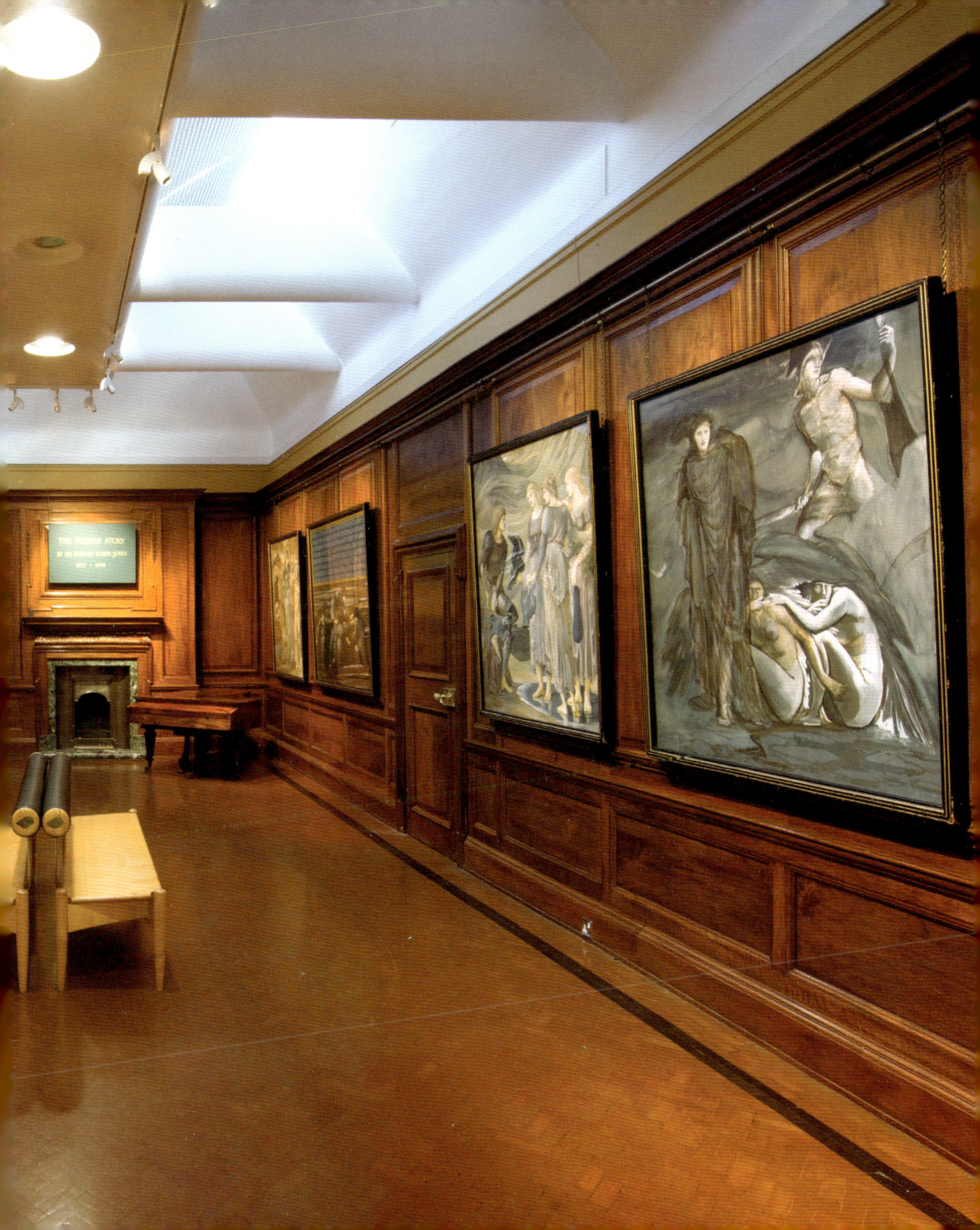

The Perseus Story

Michael Cassin

The Greek myths are a collection of stories invented by the ancients through which they attempted to make sense of the world around them. It would be a mistake to think of them in the way we think of a modern novel – as a sequence of events composed by a single author, written down and fixed forever. They were retold by word of mouth for hundreds of years and, while the basic thread of the story might remain constant, details could be varied here and there by successive narrators according to their particular interests and contemporary circumstances. Classical poets used the stories as source material; skeletons upon which to hang moral tales or theatrical tragedies; and from the earliest time, visual artists have referred to them when in need of a narrative basis for their own productions.

The Perseus legend has been one of the most popular of these heroic tales; Aeschylus, Euripides and Ovid related it in one form or another; Charles Kingsley, William Morris and Robert Graves are among those writers to retell it in modern times, there is even an opera by Richard Strauss based on the early part of the story. Its combination of excitement, violence, sensuality and ultimate morality – all the baddies eventually get their just desserts, while all the good guys live happily ever after – has made it attractive to almost all periods and all persuasions. Even the early Christians – not noted for their tolerance of the Classics – saw in the story a prefiguration of Christ's victory over the powers of evil and the foundation of a new era. In the visual arts it has provided themes for painters as varied as Titian, Correggio and Rembrandt, though perhaps the most well-known example is the bronze sculpture in Florence by Benvenuto Cellini. This gory piece shows Perseus standing over Medusa's dead body, holding aloft the terrible head with its writhing snakes and bloody, dripping neck.

The parts of the legend illustrated here by Burne-Jones are the central episodes – Perseus' search for a victory over the Gorgon Medusa, and the

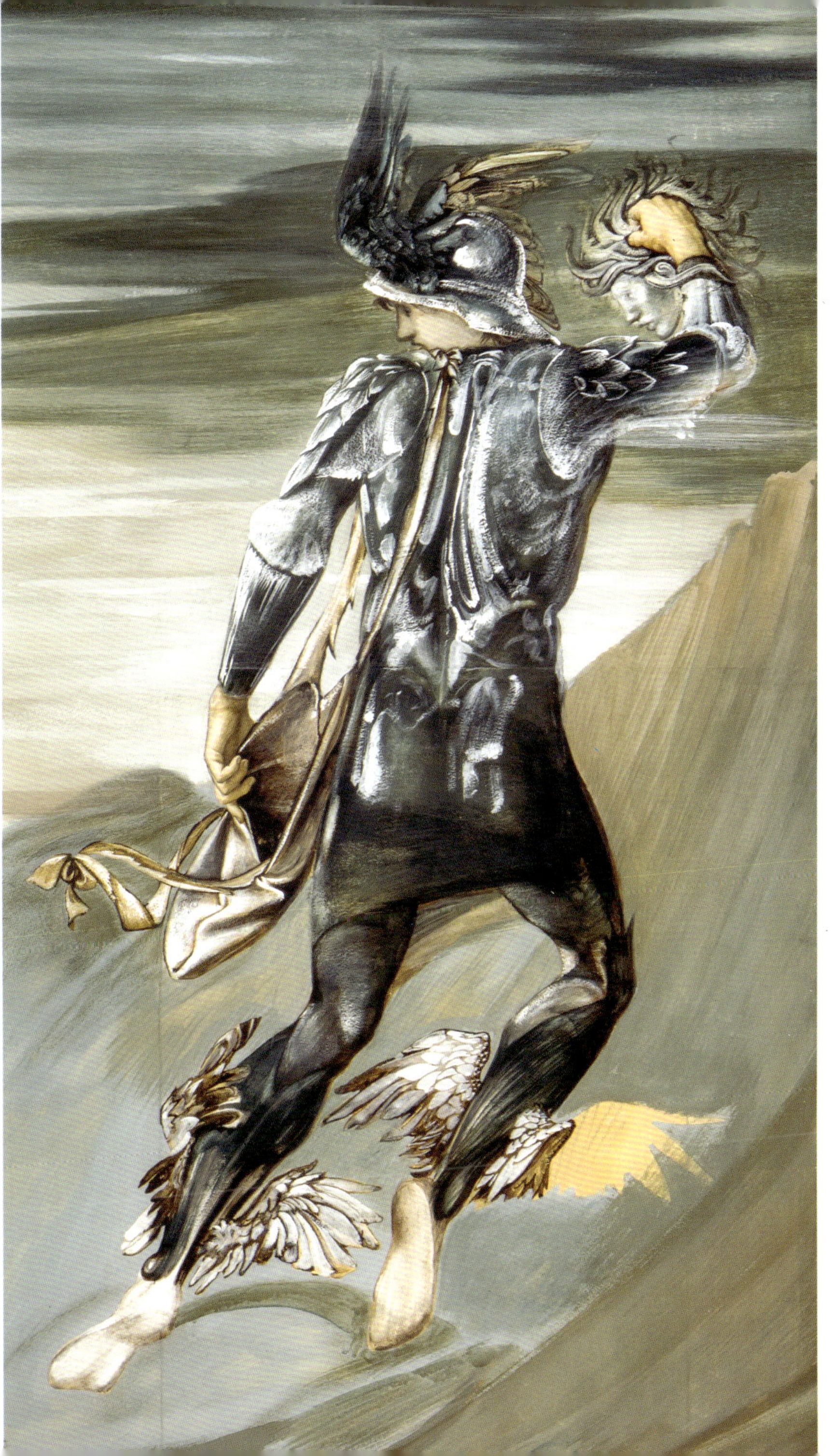

meeting with his bride Andromeda – but to understand fully what is going on it might be useful to look back briefly to the beginning of the story.

Perseus was born the son of Danaë and Zeus, the King of the Gods of Olympus. Acrisius, Danaë's father and King of Argos, had imprisoned his daughter in an impregnable subterranean chamber to prevent her ever having children as he had been told by the oracle at Delphi that his grandson would be the cause of his death. However, Zeus transformed himself into a golden rain and entered the chamber (presumably through the air vents) to fulfil his passion for Danaë, and in the course of time, she gave birth to a son. When he discovered the child, Acrisius had Danaë and Perseus locked into a chest and set adrift on the open sea, hoping that they would either drown or die of hunger and thirst, but they were released by a fisherman, Diktys, when the chest was washed up on the island of Seriphos in the Cyclades. Here Perseus grew peacefully into adolescence, until Polydectes, the King of Seriphos, jealous of the young man's physique, and anxious to seduce Danaë, plotted to remove him. The King gave a great banquet to which all those invited, Perseus among them, were required to bring a horse as a gift. Perseus, still living in the household of the fisherman Diktys, was too poor to bring such a grand present and Polydectes hoped this would shame him into leaving Seriphos. Instead, the young man arrived empty-handed, but demonstrated his honour by swearing to bring Polydectes whatever he desired, even if it were the head of Medusa. His choice of this gift is not as arbitrary as it may seem to us – in very ancient traditions Medusa is described as having the body of a horse, and she appears in that form on at least one archaic amphora (Athena is held responsible for this distressing condition, see p. 47), Perseus is, therefore, offering the head of the most 'unique' horse in existence, and the most dangerous since Medusa's appearance is terrifying – she has living snakes instead of hair and her stare turns mortal things to inanimate stone. Polydectes accepts the offer delightedly; the Gorgons live at the end of the earth, and if Perseus survives the hazardous journey he will almost certainly be petrified by Medusa's glance, and having made this declaration before the assembled guests at the feast, he would be too ashamed to return empty-handed. The King would be rid of him and Danaë would be defenceless. It is at this particular point that Burne-Jones' illustrations begin.

Characters

Acrisius: King of Argos, father of Danaë, grandfather of Perseus.

Andromeda: Daughter of Cepheus and Cassiopeia, wife of Perseus.

Athena: Goddess of wisdom and war, daughter of Zeus, patron of Perseus.

Atlas: A Titan, condemned forever to support the sky.

Cassiopeia: Wife of Cepheus, mother of Andromeda, eventually placed in the sky as a constellation.

Cepheus: King of Joppa in Ethiopia, father of Andromeda, like his wife eventually transferred to the sky as a constellation.

Chrysaor: Son of Medusa and Poseidon, born from the blood of Medusa's severed head.

Danaë: Daughter of Acrisius, seduced by Zeus, mother of Perseus.

Delphic Oracle: The most important oracle in Greece, whose predictions were famous for their ambiguity.

Diktys: A fisherman, later King of Seriphos, protector of Danaë and Perseus.

Graiae: Daughters of Phorkys, sisters of the Gorgons, grey-haired from birth, with only one eye and one tooth between them.

Hades: God of the Underworld, the land of the dead, whose helmet made anyone wearing it invisible, brother of Zeus.

Hermes: God of travellers, traders and thieves; son of Zeus and messenger of the gods, whose winged sandals were loaned to Perseus.

Medusa: Daughter of Phorkys, the only mortal one of the three Gorgons. She had offended Athena and had been turned into a hideously ugly creature with snakes instead of hair, a look so terrifying it turned people to stone and, in some accounts, the body of a horse.

Pegasus: A winged horse, the offspring of Medusa and Poseidon, born from the blood of Medusa's severed head.

Phorkys: Father of the Gorgons and the Graiae, one of the older generation of deities before Zeus and the Olympians.

Polydectes: King of the Seriphos, turned to stone by Perseus.

Poseidon: God of the sea, whose emblems were the trident and the horse. Seducer of Medusa, enemy of Athena and brother of Zeus.

Titans: A race of pre-Olympian Gods, frequently referred to as giants.

Zeus: King of the Gods of Mount Olympus, seducer of Danaë, father of Athena, Hermes and Perseus.

1

THE CALL OF PERSEUS

1877 | gouache on paper laid on linen canvas | 152.5 x 127 cm | inv. no 100

Perseus sits on the bank of a stream outside the city, naked and dejected, already regretting his impetuosity. A heavily draped figure stands over him, sympathetically holding out a hand. This is the goddess Athena who reveals herself to Perseus' startled eyes in the centre of the picture, wearing the armour traditionally associated with her (she is the goddess of wisdom, and secondarily, of war, and is said to have emerged fully armed from the head of her father Zeus). Athena has overheard the conversation at the feast, and her hatred of the Gorgons (daughters of the ancient deity Phorkys) is such that she comes to Perseus' aid. She advises him about his journey, warns him of Medusa's stony stare, and, traditionally, she lends him a highly polished shield in which he will be able to see Medusa's reflection without risking the dreadful consequences of looking at her directly (in the painting this shield has become a mirror – conveniently small and portable, and just as effective).

It is interesting to see how Burne-Jones makes use of an old-fashioned pictorial device to assist his narrative. On the one hand he is limited by the commission to ten panels, on the other he feels the need to refer to both the incidents depicted here, and so he includes both episodes in the same picture space, allowing the characters to appear twice in the same continuous landscape.

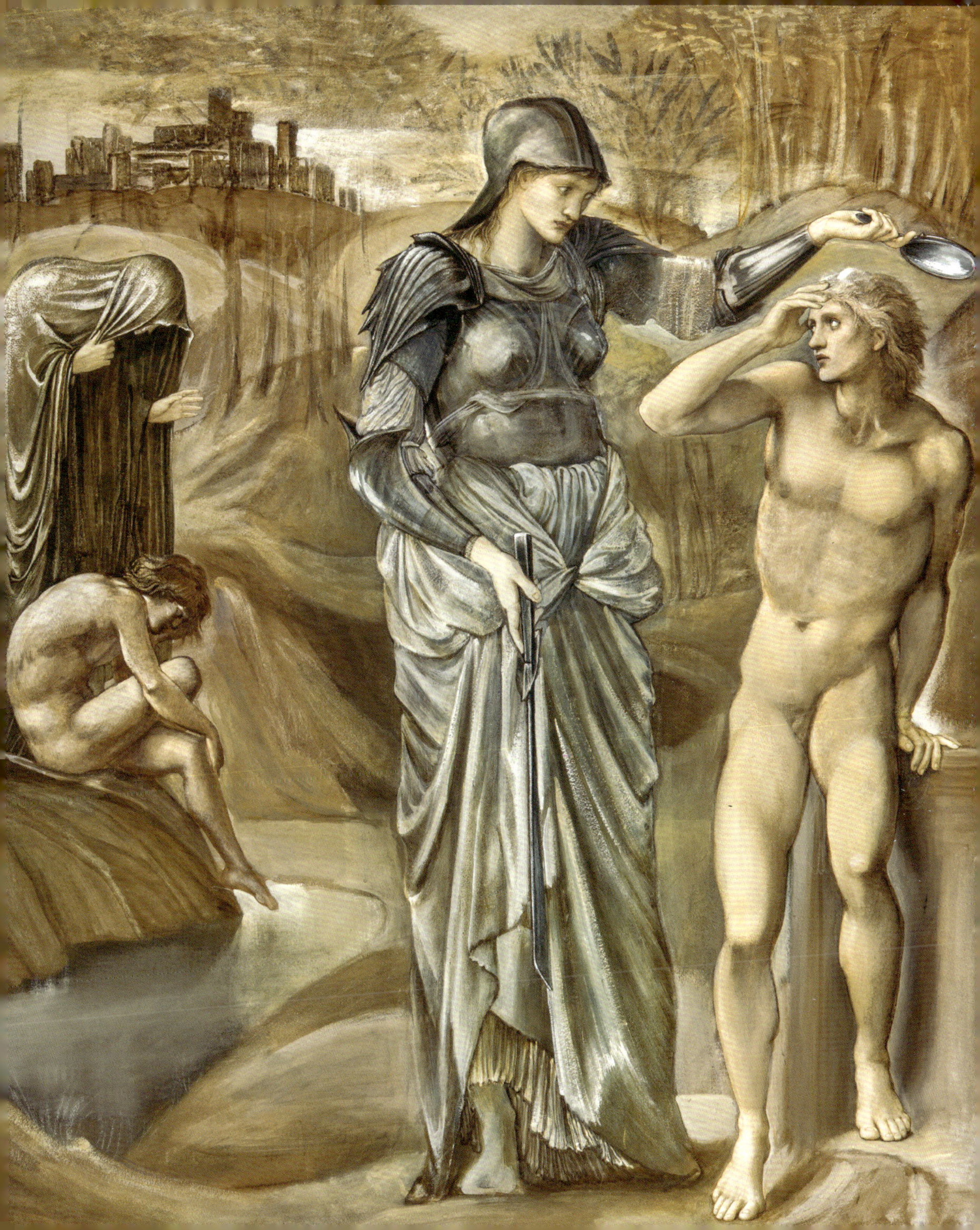

2

PERSEUS AND THE GRAIAE

*c.*1877–80 | gouache on paper laid on linen canvas | 152.5 x 170.5 cm | inv. no 101

Athena belongs to the younger generation of Greek deities, the siblings and children of Zeus. Older than this set, and more deeply rooted in the subconscious of the Greeks and other European ethnic groups are deities whose roles and powers are less clearly defined, but whom the Olympian gods never completely supplanted. The Gorgons and their sisters the Graiae are among them. The Graiae lived in a land of darkness, near the ends of the earth, as near to the east as it is to the west. They must have been an unnerving sight, for they had only one eye and one tooth between them, and passed each from one to another when it was required. They refuse to tell Perseus the whereabouts of their strange sisters and he is forced to steal their only eye while it is in transit, and hold it to ransom until he obtains the necessary information.

In this frame, Burne-Jones has included a sort of shorthand precis of the story in Latin, which effectively cuts down the area he has to work with. In the low, wide space he describes the rocky barrenness of the Graiae's uncomfortable surroundings, not far from where the earth and the sky meet. The figures crouch, their hands groping unsuccessfully, trying to retrieve their lost power of vision. He has clothed the figures in the rippling thin draperies, reminiscent of dampened cheesecloth, of which other Victorian Classicists, like Albert Moore and Lord Leighton, were so fond, and which derive from the type of costume worn by the goddesses of the Parthenon Pediment, now in the British Museum.

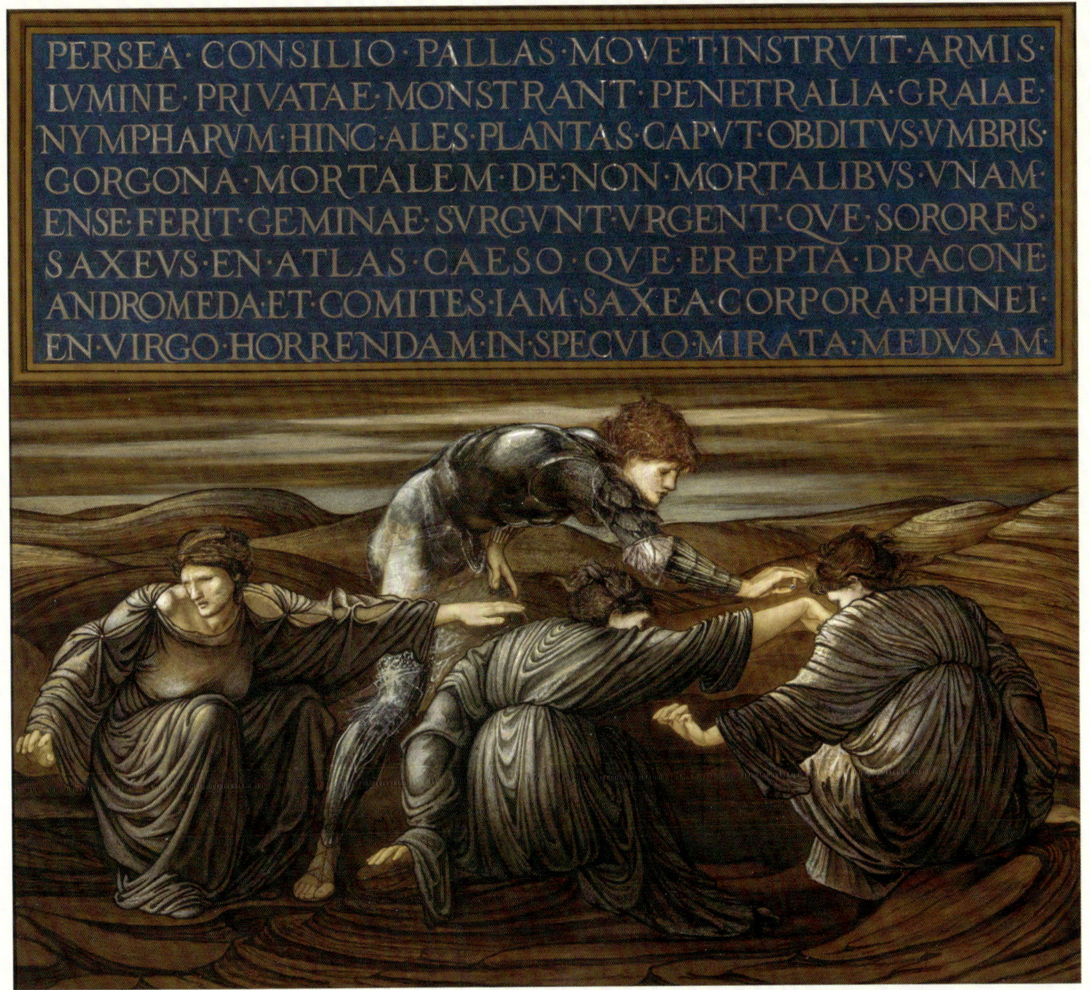

Translation: [1] *Pallas Athene with her urging spurred Perseus to action and equipped him with arms.* [2] *The blind sisters of the Gorgons revealed to him the remote home of the nymphs.* [3] *From there he went with wings on his feet and with his head shrouded in darkness, and* [4 & 5] *with his sword he struck the one Gorgon who was subject to death – the others were immortal.* [6] *Her two sisters arose and pursued him.* [7] *Next he turned Atlas to stone,* [8 & 9] *the sea serpent was slain and Andromeda rescued and the comrades of Phineus became lumps of rock.* [10] *Then Andromeda looked with wonder in a mirror at the dreadful Medusa.*

3

PERSEUS AND THE SEA NYMPHS

1877 | gouache on paper laid on linen canvas | 152.8 x 126.4 cm | inv. no 102

Perseus also visited three benign nymphs whose identity varies. The order of these visits varies too, many commentators placing this visit before that to the Graiae who live nearer to the Gorgons than to the other nymphs. The journey is a long and hazardous one and would be difficult to make without the gifts given to Perseus by the helpful nymphs shown here. It seems unlikely that Perseus would walk to the end of the earth, near the Gorgons' abode, find out from the Graiae how to negotiate the last bit of the journey and then walk all the way back to pick up his borrowed winged sandals and helmet. Sometimes they are the Stygian Nymphs who inhabit the region between the Underworld and the land of the living humans. In either case they are the guardians of a Kibisis, a magic wallet to contain the Gorgon's head, Hades' helmet of invisibility, and Hermes' handy winged sandals, all of which are loaned to Perseus through the intercession of his patroness Athena.

The landscape is as barren as that in which the Graiae live emphasising the nymphs' remoteness from the world of men, but the lighter tones suggest an atmosphere of calm quite different from the tension of the preceding scene. Their disproportionate height and languid pose enhances their elegance just as contemporary fashion designers elongate the figures of their drawings in a quite unnatural way for a supposedly elegant effect.

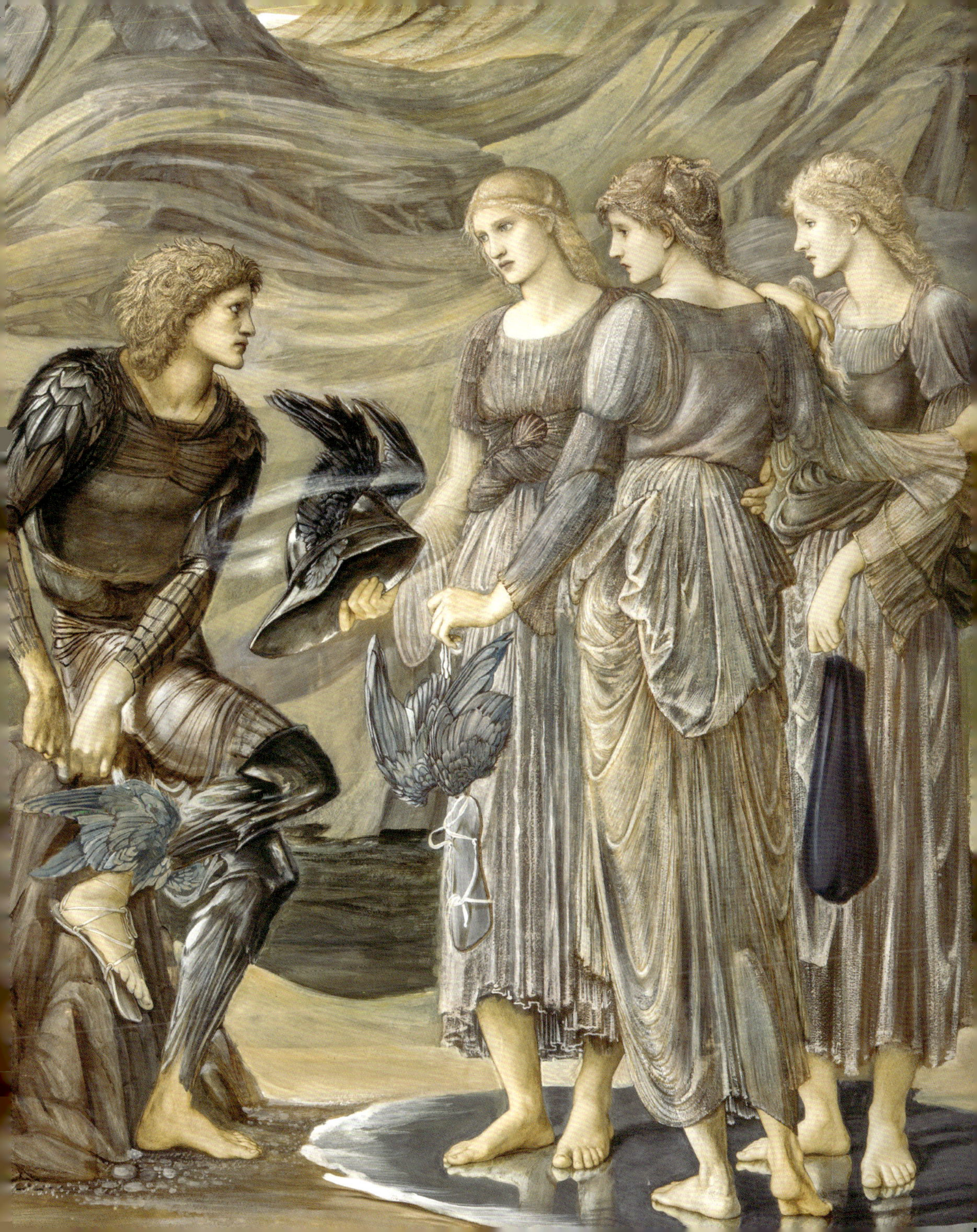

4

THE FINDING OF MEDUSA

*c.*1882 | gouache on paper laid on linen canvas | 152.5 x 137.7 cm | inv. no 103

At last Perseus arrives in the land of the Gorgons, the land of the setting sun at the western extremity of the world. He locates Medusa, the only mortal one of the sisters, in his mirror as she stands on the left, raising her hands in a vain attempt at self-protection, while her sisters crouch under their wings, only recently roused from sleep.

This is the least finished of the series, the positions of the figures only tentatively mapped in, the background an unclear suggestion with little indication of colour. The drama of the scene, however, is conveyed by the starkly contrasting light and shade, dabs of white picking out significant details from the indefinite darkness.

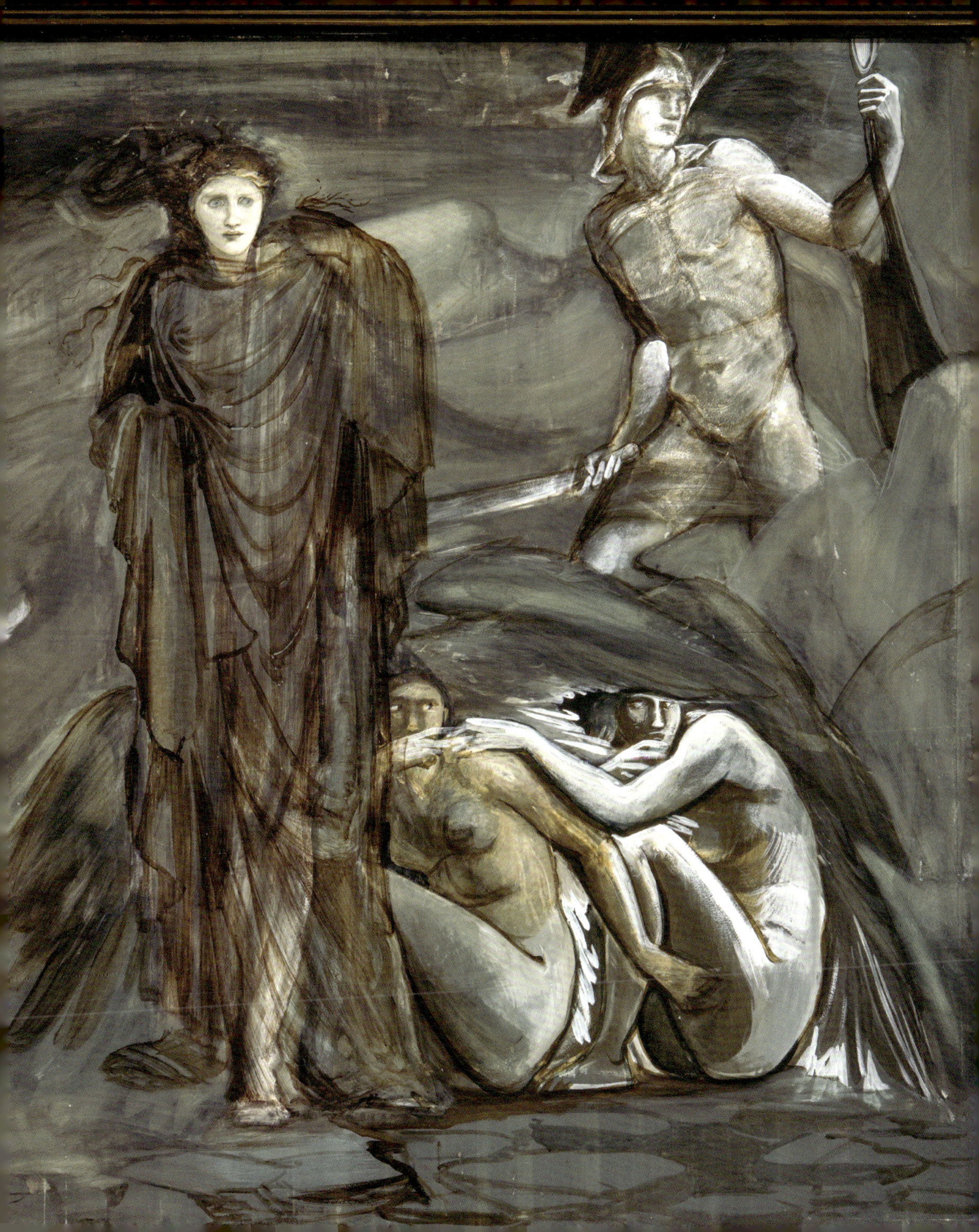

5

THE DEATH OF MEDUSA I

*c.*1882 | gouache on paper laid on linen canvas | 124.5 x 116.9 cm | inv. no 109

Unknown to Perseus, Medusa is pregnant with the children of Poseidon and when her head is severed, these children, the winged horse Pegasus, later to be tamed and ridden by Bellerophon, and Chrysaor, whose son's cattle were to provide Hercules with his tenth labour, spring fully grown from her neck. The act which resulted in this pregnancy took place inside a temple of Athena and this desecration of a place sacred to her is what engendered Athena's hatred for Medusa in the first place. In the light of this revelation it can be seen that Athena is not merely being altruistic in helping Perseus – as perhaps we thought at the beginning of the story – it happens that by helping him achieve his objective she can also use him as the instrument of her revenge.

In contrast to number 4, this is a highly finished tightly composed drawing. Severed snakes from Medusa's head drop wriggling to the floor alongside the limp, headless body. The space in the picture is shallow, sealed off at the back by a flat backcloth of pink and gold which pushes the figures out at us. Pegasus is drawn with meticulous attention to anatomy and his wings are gilded, as befits such a remarkable beast, but Chrysaor is shown without the curved golden sword from which he derives his name.

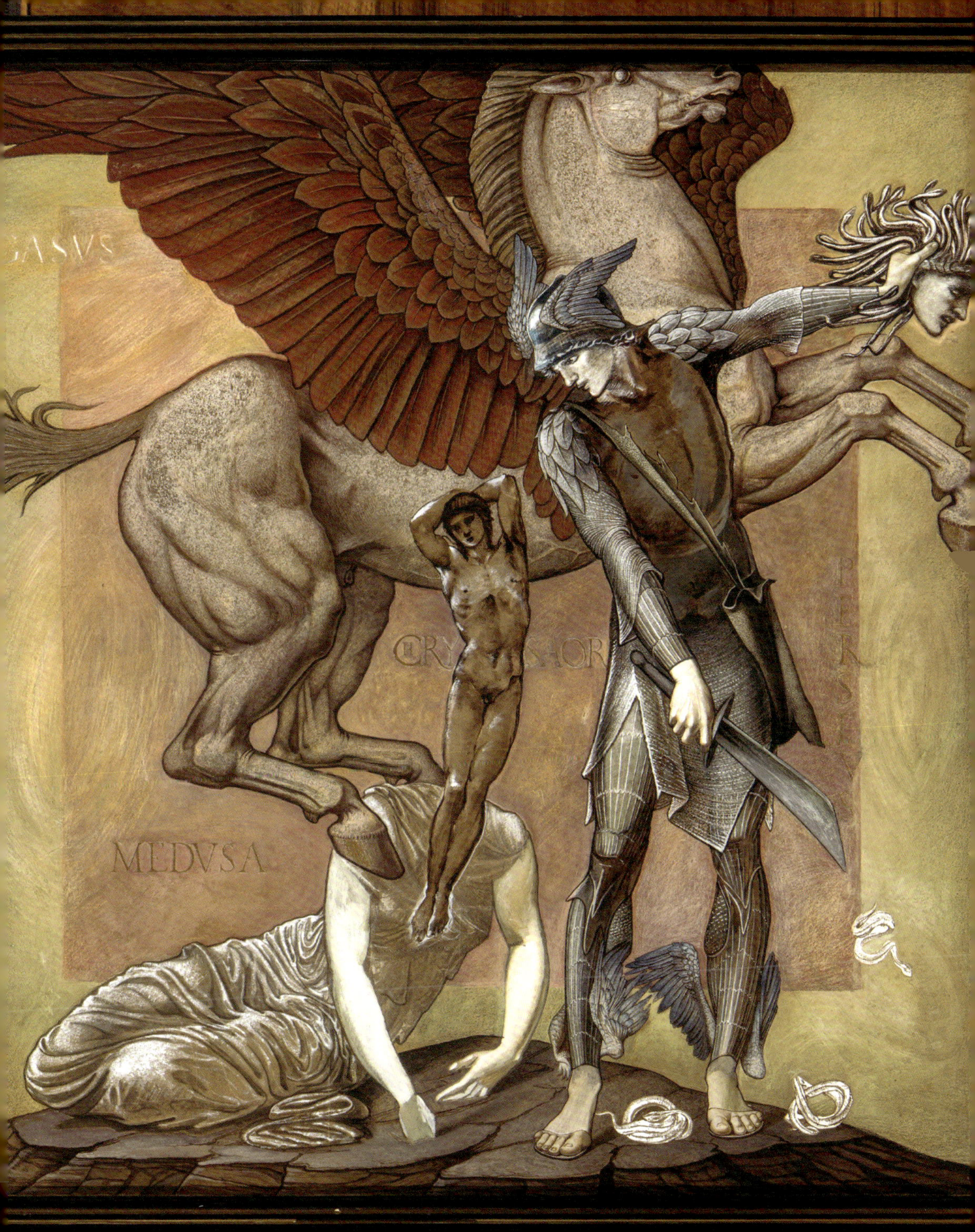
PEGASVS
MEDVSA
PERSEVS

6

THE DEATH OF MEDUSA II

*c.*1881–82 | gouache on paper laid on linen canvas | 152.5 x 136.5 cm | inv. no 104

Here the other Gorgons, fully awake now and aware of the disaster which has overtaken their sister, make a desperate attempt to follow and attack Perseus, but, aided by Hades' helmet of invisibility and Hermes' sandals, the hero disappears in the darkening clouds, placing the head into the Kibisis, for safety, and so as not to turn everything he passes into stone.

Here Burne-Jones has filled the top three-quarters of his picture with the three massive flying figures, the two startled sisters, spreading their wings on the left and Perseus making a hasty getaway behind the clouds rolling in from the bay. If we look at the brown edge at the bottom of the picture we can see evidence of the method used by the artist to transfer details from smaller preparatory sketches to these large-scale cartoons (drawings the same size as the finished painting). Squares would be drawn on top of the small drawing, and similar squares would be drawn on the blank paper prepared for the cartoon, so that when the main lines of the sketch are transferred the scale of the drawing is preserved.

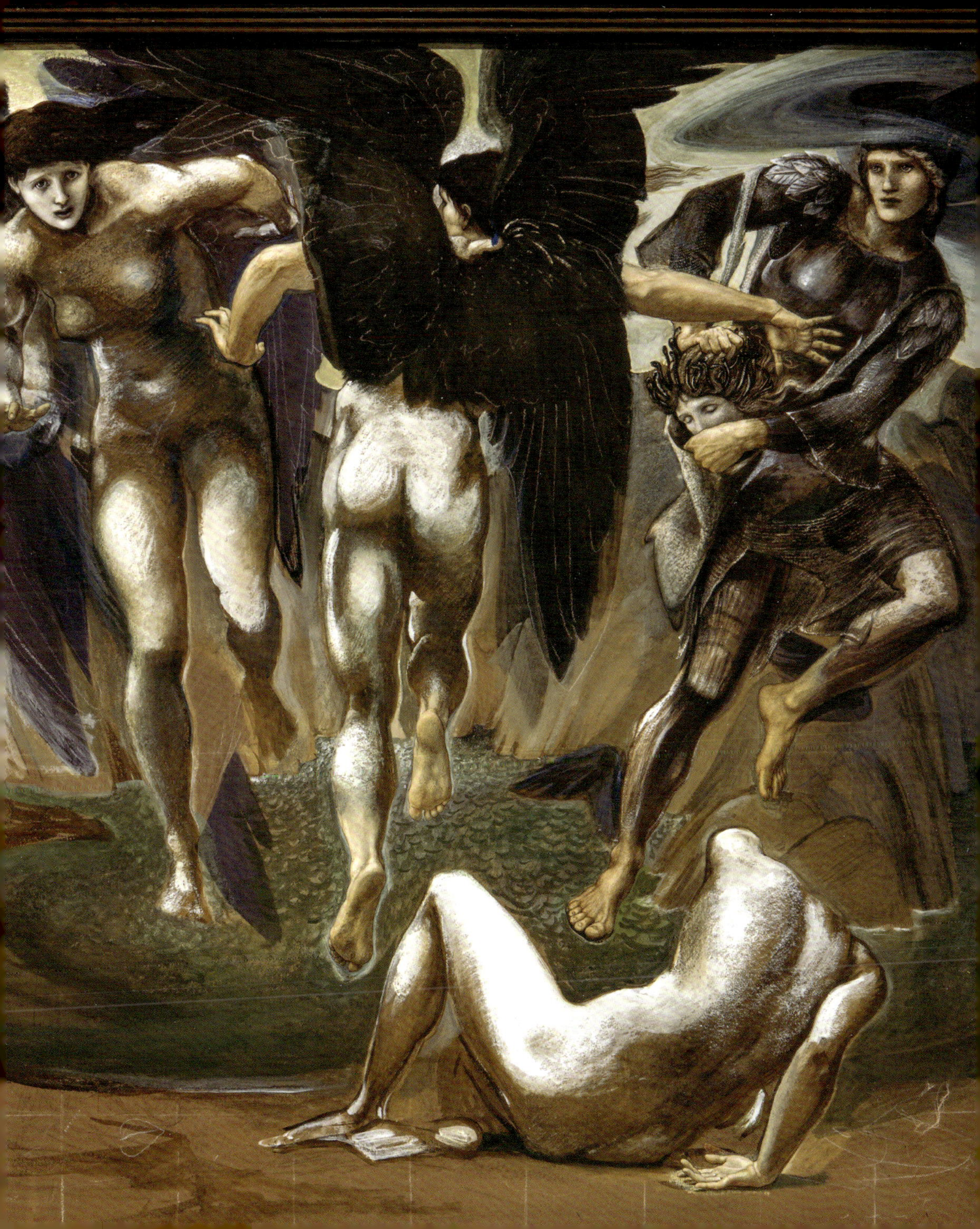

7

ATLAS TURNED TO STONE

*c.*1878 | gouache on paper laid on linen canvas | 152.5 x 190 cm | inv. no 105

As we mentioned at the beginning, myths are stories invented to explain the natural world. For the Greeks there had to be a reasonable explanation of how the sky was prevented from falling down and crushing the people of the earth. If the sky did not fall down, something somewhere must prop it up. Looking around them, the highest things known to the Greeks and their fellow inhabitants of the Mediterranean were the Atlas Mountains in North Africa, which were so high they disappeared into the sky they supported. That answers one question, but asks another: how did the mountains get there? Mountains are made of rock and stone, how did so much stone come to be piled up to such a great height? The story of Atlas tells us, Atlas was a Titan, a race of giant near-deities of a pre-Zeus generation which was defeated by Zeus and his supporters. As a punishment Atlas was condemned to stand on the earth forever holding up the sky – we can see several signs of the Zodiac in the grey Sphere resting on the giant's shoulders. When Perseus flew past, Atlas, who from his great height had seen the whole story, asked that he might be turned to stone and released from his misery and boredom (other stories tell of Atlas' lack of hospitality to the tired Perseus, for which he was petrified by Medusa's head).

The picture shows us the moment at which the giant is turned into stone, transformed into the mountain range which bears his name and supports the sky. Inevitably, nowadays, and particularly for children, this episode is reminiscent of the heroes of American comic-books, but not simply because Atlas is green like the Incredible Hulk. The receding figure of Perseus, flying off in not too confident foreshortening, is not unlike those bulging contemporary heroes Superman and Batman; he even has super-powers and an unassailable moral code to match.

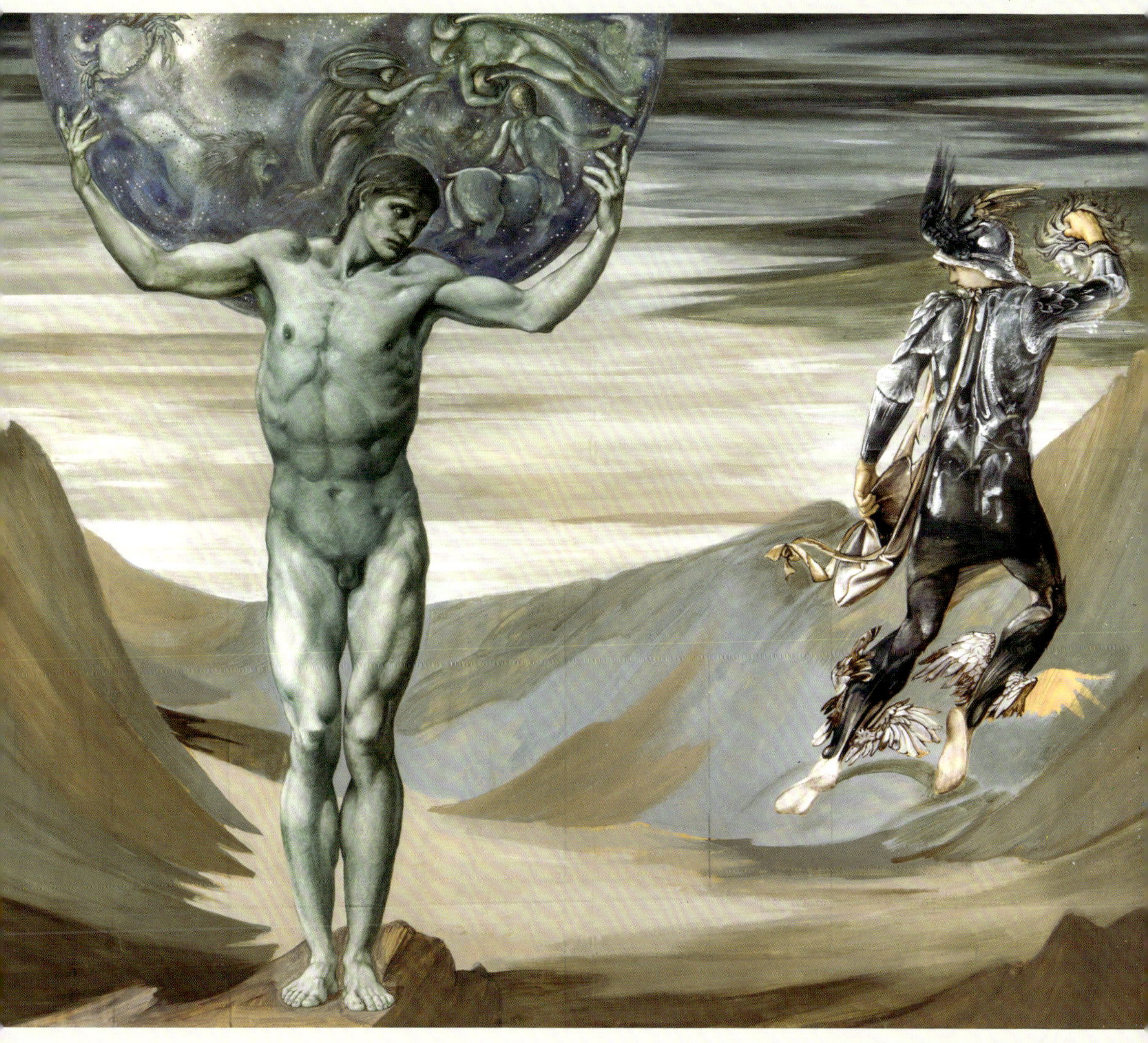

8

THE ROCK OF DOOM

*c.*1884–85 | gouache on paper laid on linen canvas | 154 x 128.6 cm | inv. no 107

To appease the god Poseidon, who had been insulted by the pride of his wife Cassiopeia, Cepheus, King of Joppa in Ethiopia, had been advised to sacrifice his daughter, Andromeda, to a sea monster sent by Poseidon to eat her. Perseus sees the beautiful girl chained to the rocky coast, falls instantly in love with her and resolves to save her from the monster.

Here we see Perseus removing Hades' helmet so that Andromeda might see him pausing in flight at the sight of such a beautiful but unusual discovery. Andromeda stands in a pose which seems remarkably relaxed for one in such dire circumstances, her head bent demurely as if to emphasise her shame at her nakedness, which is nevertheless as idealised, white and chaste, as a marble statue.

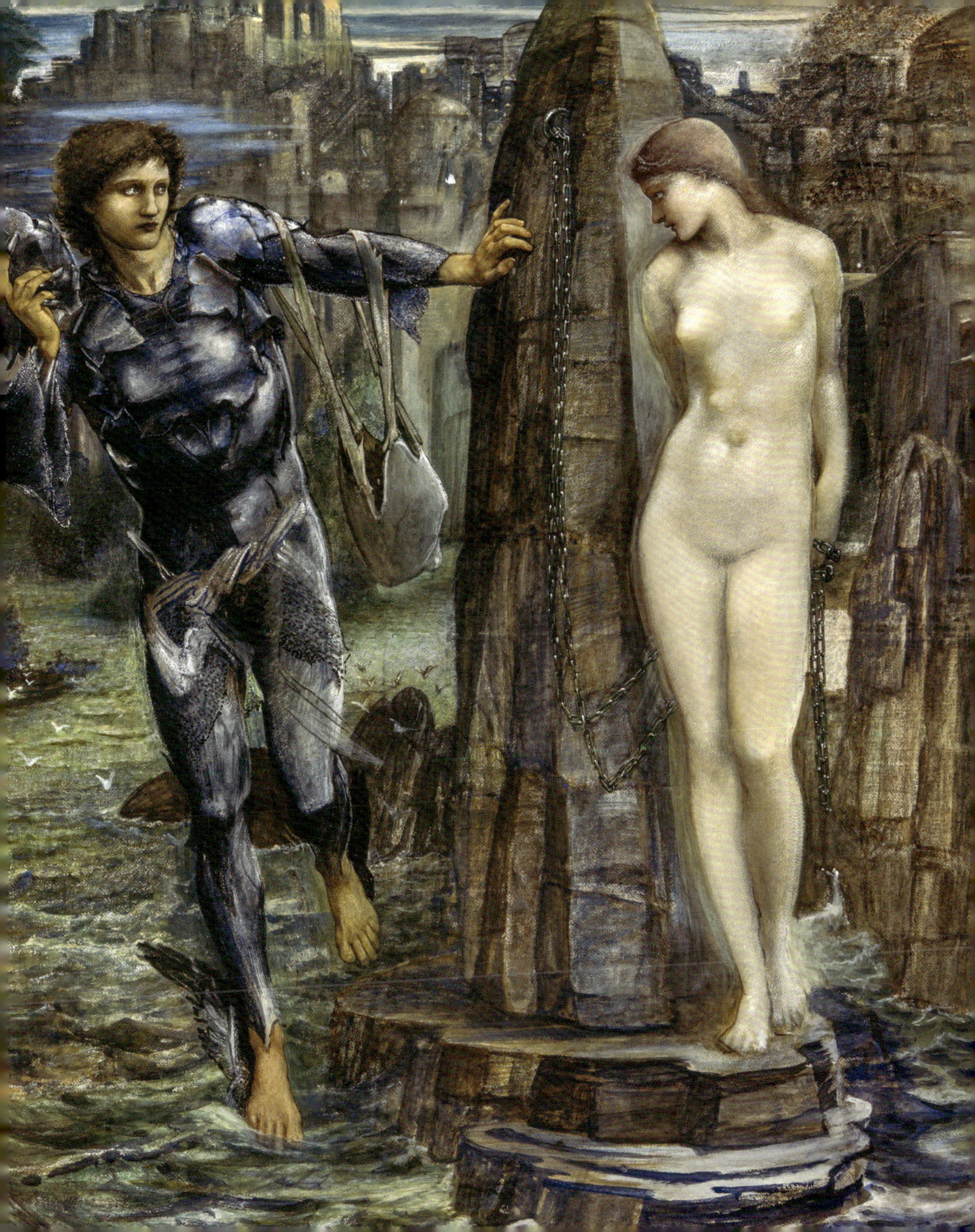

9

THE DOOM FULFILLED

c.1884–85 | gouache on paper laid on linen canvas | 153.8 x 138.4 cm | inv. no 106

Having freed Andromeda from her chains, Perseus used her as bait for the monster rather than simply flying away with her; this would bring the wrath of Poseidon down on the innocent people of the city, and since Perseus is an honourable man he feels this should be prevented. He lay in wait until the seas parted and the huge eel-like creature appeared to claim his tribute, then he emerged from his hiding-place and battled with the monster until it eventually fell dead into the water. At this point we might wonder why Perseus does not simply show the monster Medusa's head and defeat it without risk to himself. We can only conclude that he wanted to show his new girlfriend how brave and strong he was, and how much he loved her – he was showing off.

On the left we are treated to a back view of Andromeda's graceful figure, whose pose seems as unrelated to her danger as her expression. The rest of the space is given over to the violent struggle between the hero and the monster, whose body coils in sweeping arcs round Perseus to squeeze the life out of him.

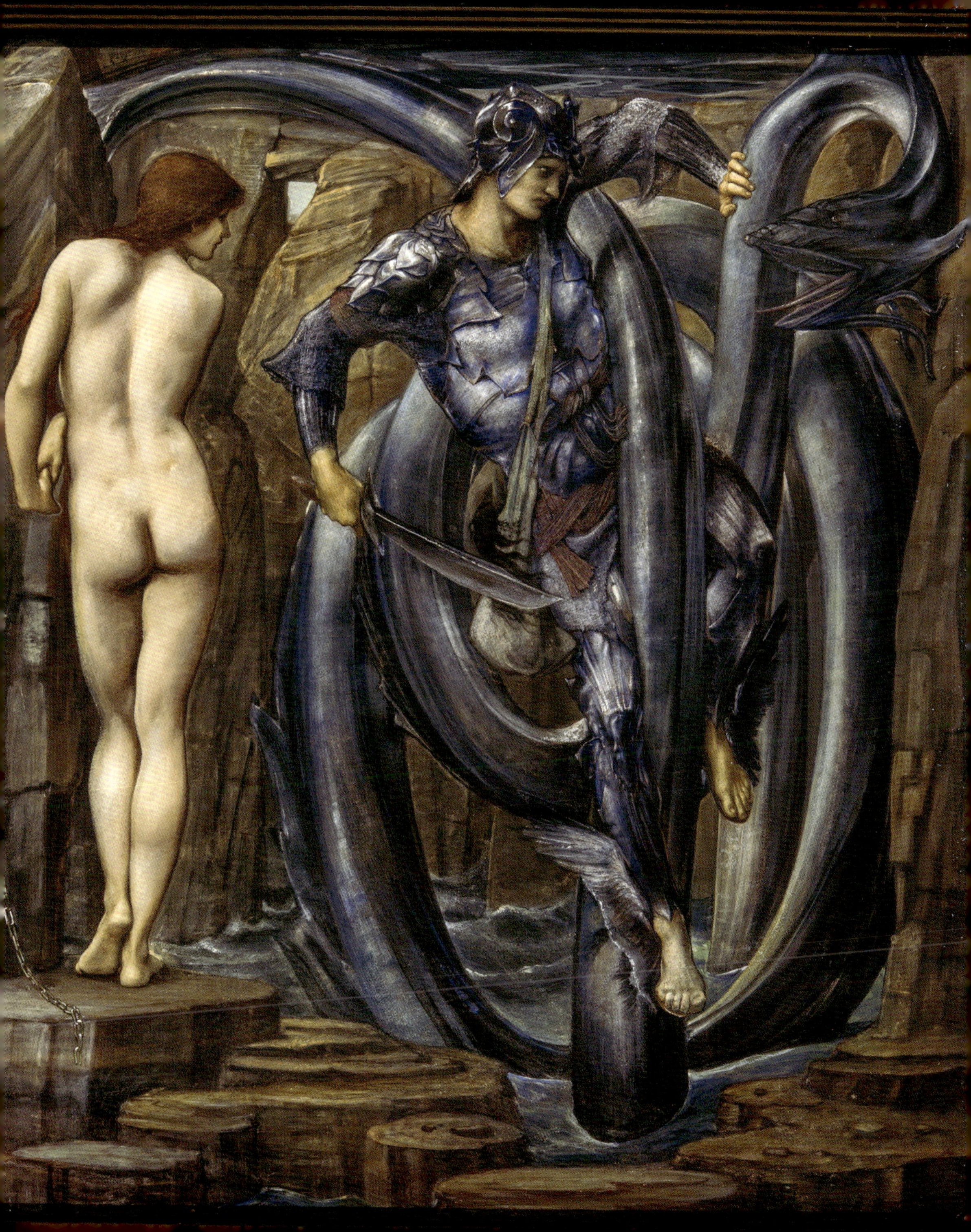

10

THE BALEFUL HEAD

1885 | gouache on paper laid on linen canvas | 153.7 x 129 cm | inv. no 108

The final picture in the series shows Perseus and Andromeda together in safety in a luxurious garden. This is presumably after their marriage – undertaken not without a certain amount of opposition from former suitors and the girl's parents – when Perseus has the time and energy to tell his story and to display to his wife the prize he has won. Still, of course, the head may not be looked at directly, and Andromeda may view it only in the safe reflection of a well's calm.

The space in the foreground is emphasised by the foreshortening of the octagonal top of the well and enclosed by the screen of foliage behind the figures. The surface of the picture is highly finished and details are carefully noted, but the picture is balanced and quiet as befits its subject matter, no wind disturbs the water or shakes the leaves from the trees, just as no disturbances remain to interrupt the couple's happiness.

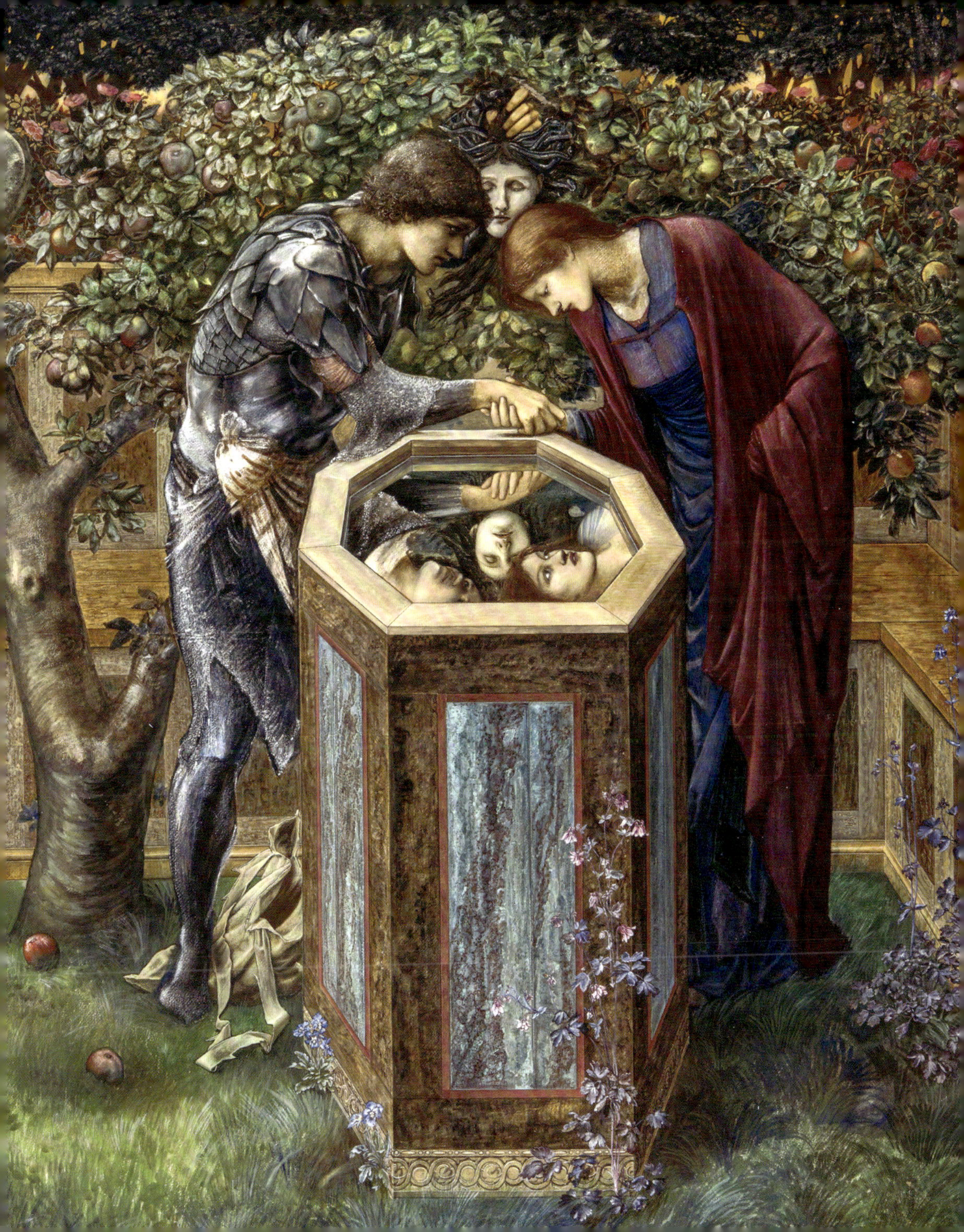

The Baleful Head is where Burne-Jones ends the series. His ten panels are complete, none of the episodes illustrated could have been omitted without disturbing the flow of the narrative, but the story does not end here. It hinges on Perseus' desire for revenge upon the evil Polydectes and is not complete until this revenge is obtained. Returning to Seriphos, Perseus found that his mother and Diktys had taken refuge in a temple to escape from the King. He went straight to the palace where he found Polydectes feasting self-indulgently (some say that the feast is the same as the one in progress when Perseus departed). He proclaimed his return, announced his gift and, when mocked in disbelief, produced the dreadful head from his magic sack, averted his eyes and turned the revellers and their king into a circle of stones which may still be seen on the island.

Properly avenged at last, he returned his borrowed weapons to the Sea Nymphs, gave the head of Medusa to Athena, who wore it from then on as part of her insignia and, placing Diktys on the throne of Seriphos, set off for Argos. His grandfather fled, fearing the consequences of Perseus' return and the hero became King in his place. Sometime later, while competing in a series of competitive games, Perseus threw a discus into the crowd of spectators, wounding an old man on the foot. On examination, the old man proved to be none other than his grandfather, Acrisius, and despite its position, the injury turned out to be fatal, thus fulfilling the prophecy made by the Delphic Oracle at the beginning of the story.

Deeply saddened by this occurrence, Perseus left Argos, but taking Andromeda with him, he founded, according to one tradition, the Greek city of Mycenae and a great dynasty from which kings of Persia claimed descent and through which they asserted their rights to the kingdoms of Greece.

The Stories of Perseus' death are indistinct and conflicting. Eventually, however, Perseus and Andromeda were placed in the heavens as constellations through the influence of the goddess Athena, presumably in recognition of services rendered, and there they remain undisturbed.

If you would like to read the full story of Perseus, and the other characters mentioned briefly here, you might refer to *The Heroes* by Charles Kingsley, or for a fully annotated version, *The Greek Myths* by Robert Graves.

Bibliography

Arscott, Caroline, *William Morris and Edward Burne-Jones: Interlacings*, New Haven and London, 2008.

Ash, Russell, *Sir Edward Burne-Jones*, New York, 1993 [*The Arming of Perseus* (Stuttgart), plate 27; *The Rock of Doom* (Stuttgart), plate 28; *The Baleful Head* (Stuttgart), plate 29].

Barringer, Tim, Jason Rosenfeld and Alison Smith, *Pre-Raphaelites Victorian Avant-Garde*, exhibition catalogue, Tate Britain, 2012 [*The Rock of Doom* (Stuggart), 172; *The Doom Fulfilled* (Stuggart), 173; *The Baleful Head* (Stuggart), 174].

Bell, Malcolm, *Sir Edward Burne-Jones A Record and Review*, London, 4th edition 1898, [*The Call of Perseus*; *The Baleful Head*].

Bullen, J.B., *The Pre-Raphaelite Body: Fear and Desire in Painting, Poetry, and Criticism*, Oxford, 1998.

Cecil, David, *Visionary and Dreamer: Samuel Palmer and Edward Burne-Jones*, London, 1969 [*The Doom Fulfilled*, plate 54].

Cheney, Liana De Girolami, 'Edward Burne-Jones' "Andromeda": Transformation of Historical and Mythological Sources', *Artibus et Historiae*, vol. 25, no. 49 (2004), pp. 197–227, [*The Rock of Doom*, p. 198; *The Doom Fulfilled*, p. 198; *The Baleful Head*, p. 199].

Christian, John, *Edward Burne-Jones*, exhibition catalogue, Arts Council of Great Britain, 1975 [*The Arming of Perseus*, no. 162; *The Baleful Head* (Stuttgart), no. 173].

Conrad, Christofer, Annabel Zettel (eds), *Edward Coley Burne-Jones, The Earthly Paradise*, exhibition catalogue, Staatsgalerie Stuttgart, 2009.

Cruise, Colin, *Pre-Raphaelite Drawing*, exhibition catalogue, Birmingham Museum and Art Gallery, 2011.

Fitzgerald, Penelope, *Edward Burne-Jones: A Biography*, London, 1975 [*Perseus and the Graiae*, p. 24; *The Finding of Medusa*, p. 24].

Flanders, Judith, *A Circle of Sisters: Alice Kipling, Georgiana Burne-Jones, Agnes Poynter and Louisa Baldwin*, London, 2001.

Harrison, Martin and Waters, Bill, *Burne-Jones*, London, 1973 [*The Call of Perseus*, p. 119; *Perseus and the Graiae*, p. 120; *Perseus and the Sea Nymphs*, p. 113; *The Finding of Medusa*, p.112; *The Death of Medusa I*, p. 119; *The Death of Medusa II*].

Ironside, Robin and Gere, John, *Pre-Raphaelite Painters*, London, 1948 [*The Call of Perseus*, plate 85; *The Arming of Perseus*, plate 84].

Johnson, May, *Burne-Jones: All Colour Paperback*, London and New York, 1979.

Kestner, J., 'Burne-Jones and Nineteenth Century Misogyny', *Biography: An Interdisciplinary Quarterly*, 1984 [*The Death of Medusa*, p. 109; *The Rock of Doom*, pp. 111–2; *The Doom Fulfilled*, pp. 111–4; *The Baleful Head*, pp. 115–6].

Kestner, Joseph, *Mythology and Misogyny: The Social Discourse of Nineteenth Century British Classical-Subject Painting*, Madison, Wisconsin, 1989 [*Study for The Calling of Perseus*, p. 127; *Study for Chrysaor for The Birth of Chrysaor*, p. 127; *Study for The Doom Fulfilled*, p. 128; *The Calling of Perseus* (Stuttgart), p. 128; *Perseus and the Graiae* (Stuttgart), p. 129; *The Nymphs Arming Perseus* (Stuttgart), p. 129; *The Finding of Medusa* (Stuttgart), p. 130; *The Birth of Chrysaor* (Southampton), p. 130; *The Death of Medusa* (Stuttgart), p. 313; *The Rock of Doom* (Stuttgart), p. 131; *The Doom Fulfilled* (Stuttgart), p. 132; *The Baleful Head* (Stuttgart), p.132].

Korb, Elisa and Tessa Sidey, *Hidden Burne-Jones Works on paper by Edward Burne-Jones from Birmingham Museums and Art Gallery*, London, 2007 [*Study of Perseus in Armour for 'The Finding of Medusa'; Study of Wings for 'The Death of Medusa'; Sketchbook – Nude Study of Medusa for 'The Death of Medusa I'; Sketchbook – The Perseus Series – Head Studies of Medusa and Perseus; Sketchbook – The Perseus Series – Nude Studies for 'Perseus Slaying the Sea-Monster'; Sketchbook – The Perseus Series – Study for 'Perseus Slaying Sea Monster' or 'Doom Fulfilled'; Sketchbook – Study for the Head of Perseus; Sketchbook – Studies of Figures for 'The Court of Phineus'*], www.preraphaelites.org.

Lewis, Wyndham, 'Art: The Brotherhood', *The Listener*, 22 April 1948 [*The Death of Medusa II*, pp. 672–3].

Lisle, Fortunée de, *Burne-Jones*, London, 1904

[*The Call of Perseus*, p. 130; *Perseus and the Sea Nymphs*, p. 131; *The Finding of Medusa*, p. 131].

Löcher, Kurt, *Der Perseus-Zyklus von Edward Burne-Jones*, Stuttgart, 1973 [*The Call of Perseus*, 1D, p. 25; *Perseus and the Graiae*, 2D, p. 36; *Perseus and the Sea Nymphs*, 3E, p. 43; *The Finding of Medusa*, 4E, p. 56; *The Death of Medusa I*, 5C, b&w repro. p.66; *The Death of Medusa II*, 6F, p. 72; *Atlas Turned to Stone*, 7D, p. 86; *The Rock of Doom*, 8P, p. 91; *The Doom Fulfilled*, 9H, p. 103; *The Baleful Head*, 11S, p. 136].

MacCarthy, Fiona, *The Last Pre-Raphaelite: Edward Burne-Jones and the Victorian Imagination*, London, 2011 [*The Perseus Series*, pp. 271–74].

Moffatt, James, 'Mr Balfour as a Man of Letters', *The Bookman*, London, August 1912, pp. 193–201 [photographs of some of the oil paintings, now in Stuttgart, in Balfour's home].

Morgan, Hilary and Peter Nahum, *Burne-Jones, The Pre-Raphaelites and their Century*, London, 1989, vol. I, 'The Text' [*Perseus Series*, pp. 75–77, nos. 56–59], vol. II, 'The Plates' [40–43].

Prettejohn, Elizabeth, *The Art of the Pre-Raphaelites*, London and Princeton, 2000.

Rose, Andrea, *The Pre-Raphaelites*, Oxford, 1977.

Spalding, Frances, *Magnificent Dreams: Burne-Jones and the Late Victorians*, Oxford, 1978, [*Perseus and the Graiae*, slip-cover].

Treuherz, Julian, 'The Pre-Raphaelites and Medieval Manuscripts' in Leslie Parris (ed), *Pre-Raphaelite Papers*, London, 1984 [*The Baleful Head*, p. 167].

Wildman and John Christian, *Edward Burne-Jones: Victorian Artist-Dreamer*, exhibition catalogue, Metropolitan Museum of Art, New York, 1998 [*The Call of Perseus*, 88; *Perseus and the Graiae*, 89; *Perseus and the Sea Nymphs (The Arming of Perseus)*, 90; *The Finding of Medusa*, 91; *The Death of Medusa I*, 92; *The Death of Medusa II*, 93; *Atlas Turned to Stone*, 94; *The Rock of Doom*, 95; *The Doom Fulfilled*, 96; *The Baleful Head*, 97. pp. 221–233].

Wilton, Andrew and Robert Upstone (eds), *The Age of Rossetti, Burne-Jones and Watts Symbolism in Britain 1860–1910*, exhibition catalogue, Tate Gallery, 1997 [*The Call of Perseus; Perseus and the Graiae; Perseus and the Nereids*, 93, p. 227; *The Finding of Medusa; The Death of Medusa (The Birth of Pegasus and Chyrsaor); Perseus Pursued by the Gorgons*, 94, p. 227; *Atlas Turned to Stone; The Rock of Doom and the Doom Fulfilled; The Court of Phineas; The Baleful Head*, 95, p. 228].

Wood, Christopher, *Burne-Jones: The Life and Works of Sir Edward Burne-Jones (1833–1898)*, London, 1999 [*The Arming of Perseus, Perseus Slaying the Serpent, Perseus and Medusa* and *The Escape of Perseus*, p. 123].

Notes: A painter of souls

1. Christian, John, *Edward Burne-Jones*, exhibition catalogue, Arts Council of Great Britain, 1975, p. 11.

2. J.J. Tissot's *The Captain's Daughter*, in the Southampton City Art Gallery collection, provides a good example of this type of painting, characterised by John Ruskin as merely tinted photographs.

3. William Gaunt, *The Aesthetic Adventure*, London, 1945, pp. 93 and 212.

4. See Penelope Fitzgerald, *Edward Burne-Jones: A Biography*, London, 1975, reprinted 1997; Martin Harrison and Bill Waters, *Burne-Jones*, London, 1973; John Dixon Hunt, *The Pre-Raphaelite Imagination 1848–1900*, London, 1968; David Cecil, *Visionary and Dreamer: Two Poetic Painters – Samuel Palmer and Edward Burne-Jones*, London, 1969; Frances Spalding, *Magnificent Dreams: Burne-Jones and the late Victorians*, Oxford, 1978.

5. Geoffrey Gait Harpham, *On the Grotesque: Strategies of Contradiction in Art and Literature*, Princeton, N.J., 1982, p.43.

6. John Ruskin, *The Art of England:* Lecture 2 – Mythic Schools of Painting – Burne-Jones and G.F. Watts, 1883, London, 1898, pp.55-56. G.F. Watts, who greatly influenced the younger Burne-Jones during the 1860s, also used myths and legends to explore human experience and values.

7. Henry James, 'London Pictures 1882', in J.L. Sweeney, *The Painter's Eye: notes and essays on the pictorial arts by Henry James*, London, 1956, p.205.

8. Burne-Jones visited Italy in 1859, 1862, 1871 and 1817. Lochner has compared the pose of Perseus in *Perseus and the Sea Nymphs* to Michelangelo's 'ignudi' on the Sistine Chapel ceiling which Burne-Jones studied on his visit to Rome in 1871.

9. Burne-Jones' fixation with reflective surfaces is amply illustrated in *The Baleful Head*. Here the unbroken surface of the water reflects the alter-ego of Woman, revealing the darker side of human nature. Truherz has identified this central motif as a Narcissus miniature adapted from an illumination in a fifteenth-century 'Roman de Rose' manuscript in the British Museum (Julian Truherz, 'The Pre-Raphaelites and Medieval Manuscripts' in Leslie Parris (ed) *Pre-Raphaelite Papers*, London, 1984, p. 167).

10. Ernst Gassirer, *Language and Myth*, quoted in James Luther Adams and Wilson Yates, *The Grotesque in Art and Literature: Theological Reflections*, Grand Rapids, Michigan/Cambridge, 1997, p 42.

11. Ruskin and Morris both promoted a 'moral aestheticism' which perceived art as a means of improving Victorian society. See Linda Dowling, *The Vulgarisation of Art: the Victorians and Aesthetic Democracy*, Richmond, Virginia, 1996.

12. Charles Taylor, *Sources of the Self: the Making of Modern Identity* 1989, Harvard, pp. 408–9.

13. Morris, *Works*, 23: 168, quoted in Dowling, p. 51.

14. A.W. Baldwin, *The Macdonald Sisters*, London, 1960, pp. 142–43.

15. Edward Henry Knight, *Reports of the United States commissioners to the Paris exposition*, 5 vols, Washington 1878, IV, p. 45.

16. Dowling, p. xii. See *The Golden Stairs* and *King Cophetua and the Beggar Maid* both in Tate Britain.

17. Morris, *Works*, 22: 165, quoted Dowling, p. 50.

18. As expressed by Baudelaire, 'The principal source of interest (of the work of art) derives from the soul (of the artist) and irresistibly reaches the soul of the onlooker', quoted from Henri Dorra, *Symbolist Art Theories: A Critical Anthology*, Berkeley, 1994, p. 6.

19. Dowling, pp. 96–97.

20. *The Art Journal*, 1878, p. 155.

21. Octave Mirbeau, 'Les Artistes de Tame', *Le Journal*, February 23, 1896, quoted in Dorra, p. 278.

22. Henry James, 'London Pictures, 1882', in Sweeney, p. 206.

23. James, 'The Picture Season in London, 1878', in Sweeney, p. 163.

24. Jane Abdy and Charlotte Gere, *The Souls An Elite in English Society 1885–1930*, London: Sidgwick & Jackson, 1984, p. 181.

25. Christie's sale on 16th July 1930, a few months after Balfour's death, was the first in a series of

auctions. Balfour's wealth came from India, his grandfather having amassed a large fortune as a contractor. With these proceeds the Whittingeham estate, in East Lothian, was acquired, on which arose a grand Neo-classical mansion designed by Robert Smirke. Balfour inherited Whittingeham when he came of age, his father having died in 1856.

26. Quoted from *England* (1892), Abdy and Gere, p. 35.

27. Abdy and Gere, p. 18.

28. Ibid., p. 31.

29. Algernon Cecil, Balfour's entry in the *Dictionary of National Biography*, quoted in Abdy and Gere, p. 35.

30. Ibid.

31. Arthur Balfour, *The Foundations of Belief*, London and Bombay, 1902, p. 31.

32. Blanche Dugdale, *Balfour*, 2 vols, London, 1936, quoted in Abdy and Gere, p. 36.

33. Abdy and Gere, p. 41.

34. Arthur James, 1st Earl of Balfour, *Chapters of Autobiography*, London, 1930, p. 233.

35. Fiona MacCarthy, *The Last Pre-Raphaelite: Edward Burne-Jones and the Victorian Imagination*, London, 2011, p. 271.

36. Balfour, *Chapters of Autobiography*, p. 233.

37. MacCarthy, p. 271.

38. Ibid., p. 274.

39. Philip Burne-Jones, 'Notes on Some Unfinished Works of Sir Edward Burne-Jones, Bt., by His Son', *Magazine of Art*, vol. 24, 1900, (pp. 159–67) p. 162.

40. Penelope Fitzgerald, *Edward Burne-Jones*, London, 1975, p. 161.

41. Letter to Arthur Balfour 27 March 1875, Balfour Papers, British Museum, Add MSS 49838.

42. Ibid.

43. MacCarthy, p. 274.

44. The gesso-specialist Osmund Weeks collaborated on the project.

45. Fitzgerald, p. 204.

46. The third gesso panel was to be *Atlas Turned to Stone* and the last *The Court of Phineus*, which would have featured as the penultimate scene preceding *The Baleful Head*.

47. Georgiana Burne-Jones, *Memorials of Edward Burne-Jones*, vol. 2, London, 1906, p. 58.

48. Elisa Korb and Tessa Sidey, *Hidden Burne-Jones Works on paper by Edward Burne-Jones from Birmingham Museums and Art Gallery*, London, 2007. *Sketchbook – Nude Study of Medusa for 'The Death of Medusa 1'*; *The Perseus Series – Head Studies of Medusa and Perseus*; *The Perseus Series – Nude Studies for Perseus Slaying the Sea-Monster*; *The Perseus Series – Study for Perseus Slaying Sea Monster or Doom Fulfilled*; *Study for the Head of Perseus*; *Studies of Figures for The Court of Phineus* (www.preraphaelites.org). Studies for *The Perseus Series* can be found in the Fitzwilliam Museum, Cambridge; the British Museum; Tate Britain; the Victoria and Albert Museum; the Courtauld Gallery, London; Manchester Art Gallery; the Whitworth Art Gallery, Manchester; the Ashmolean Museum, Oxford, and the Lady Lever Art Gallery in Port Sunlight, as well as the Art Gallery of South Australia in Adelaide, Harvard, the Statens Museum for Kunst in Copenhagen, and elsewhere.

49. MacCarthy, p. 273.

50. GBJ, *Memorials*, p. 61.

51. Letter to Helen Mary Gaskell, January 1893 quoted Fitzgerald, p. 82.

52. Fitzgerald, p. 183.

53. John Christian, 'Cat. 109, *The Golden Stairs*' in *Edward Burne-Jones Victorian Artist-Dreamer*, exhibition catalogue, Metropolitan Museum of Art, New York, 1998, p. 248. See also Anne Anderson, 'Soul's Beauty: Burne-Jones and the Girls on The Golden Stairs', *19th Century*, vol. 18, no. 1, Spring 1998, pp. 17–23.

54. Cosmo Monkhouse, Introduction to *Drawings and Studies of Edward Burne-Jones*, Burlington Fine Arts Club Exhibition, London, 1899, p. x.

55. Baldwin, p. 142.

56. Sketches of Frances Horner were sold through Christie's, London on 5 November 1993 (lot 120, 371 x 273 mm) and 10 March 1995 (lot 156, 597 x 445 mm).

57. Frances Graham, Lady Horner, *Time Remembered*, London: Heinemann, 1933, p. 26.

58. John Christian, 'Cat. 107. *Frances Graham*', in *Edward Burne-Jones Victorian Artist-Dreamer*, p. 244.

59. GBJ, *Memorials*, pp. 130–31.

60. Abdy and Gere, p. 127.

61. Martin Harrison and Bill Walters, *Burne-Jones*, London, 1989, p. 113. For an interpretation of *The Finding of Medusa* and *The Death of Medusa II*, as a product of sexual repression see Joseph Kestner, *Mythology and Misogyny: The Social Discourse of Nineteenth Century British Classical-Subject Painting*, Madison, Wisconsin, 1989, pp. 130–31.

62. Fitzgerald, p. 83.

63. Ibid.

64. GBJ, *Memorials*, p. 80.

65. Ibid., p. 81.

66. His wife Venetia Benson, the daughter of the watercolourist Alfred William Hunt, also inspired Burne-Jones.

67. GBJ, *Memorials*, pp. 145–6.

68. Simon Reynolds, *William Blake Richmond An Artist's Life 1842–1921*, Norwich, 1995, p. 45.

69. Scott Thomas Buckle, 'Is this the face of Alessandro di Marco? The forgotten features of a well-known Italian model', *British Art Journal*, vol. XIII, no. 2, (pp. 3–11) p. 7.

70. Harrison and Walters, p. 119.

71. Philip Burne-Jones, p. 159.

72. Fiona Mann, 'A Born Rebel: Edward Burne-Jones and watercolour painting 1857-80', *The Burlington Magazine*, vol. CLVI, October 2014, p. 664.

73. Roberson Archive HKI MS 248–1993, p. 178, quoted ibid.

74. 'Grosvenor Gallery Gems', *Punch*, vol. 102, May 14, 1887, p. 238.

75. *Perseus and the Graiae* was not completed until 1892, being sent to the Paris Salon in 1893.

76. Fitzgerald, p. 216.

77. Cosmo Monkhouse, 'Fine Art. The New Gallery', *Academy*, June 2, 1881, p. 383.

78. M.M. Spielmann, 'Current Art', *The Magazine of Art*, vol. 11, 1888, p. 300.

79. Willie Bridgeman, quoted in Abdy and Gere, p. 39.

80. William Graham Robertson, *Time Was: Reminiscences of W. Graham* Robertson, London: Hamish Hamilton, 1931, p. 76.

81. *Exhibition of Drawings and Studies by Sir Edward Burne-Jones, Bart*, London: Burlington Fine Arts Club, 1899, xv.

82. According to the provisions in his will the 'unfinished' paintings in his studio were sold at Christie's on 16th and 18th July 1898. Two unfinished oils, *The Death of Medusa* and *Perseus and Andromeda* were listed, but the watercolour series does not appear. See: Malcolm Bell, *Sir Edward Burne-Jones, A Record and Review*, London: G. Bell & Sons, 1910, pp. 132–33. According to Philip Burne-Jones *The Perseus Series* could still be seen in the garden studio in 1900; 'Notes on Some Unfinished Works', p. 159.

83. Bought for 1650 guineas at the William Graham sale (1886).

84. Information from the Buscot/Faringdon archives kindly supplied by Roger Vlitos, curator at Buscot Park through Alison Smith, Chief Curator at the National Portrait Gallery.

85. As above.

86. Henderson was in residence from 1887 to 1904. The Faringdon Collection is now housed at 28 Brompton Square, a property acquired by the 2nd Lord Faringdon as his London home in 1953.

87. The house was built by Henrietta, wife of the 1st Earl of Pomfret during her widowhood, between 1756 and 1759 by Stiff Leadbetter. Information from the Buscot/Faringdon archives kindly supplied by Roger Vlitos, curator at Buscot Park through Alison Smith.

88. This startling price had been negotiated on Burne-Jones's behalf by his patron William Graham.

89. Bell, p. 63.

90. *Buscot Park and the Faringdon Collection*, Buscot Park: Trustees of the Faringdon Collection, 2004, pp. 28–29.

91. December 1934 Chipperfield Bequest Fund, advisor Sir Kenneth Clark, director, National Gallery, London. The series was sold through Sotheby's on 13 June 1934 and purchased by Lady Violet. Lady Violet retired to Barnsley Park, Gloucestershire. Perhaps finding no suitable place for them, she decided to sell them. Information from the Buscot/Faringdon archives kindly supplied by Roger Vlitos, curator at Buscot Park, through Alison Smith.

Acknowledgements

Southampton City Art Gallery would like to thank the following organisations for their support in relation to *The Perseus Series*, both for the conservation of the frames, glazing of the works with Optium Museum (low reflective, UV-eliminating glazing) and publication of this book: Andrew Lloyd Webber Foundation; FoSMAG (Friends of Southampton's Museums, Archives and Galleries); TruVue.

The gallery would also like to thank the following: Anne Anderson; Andy Ball; Michael Cassin; Tim Craven; Ritchie Gooding; Ben Hall; Josef Hill; Joe Low; Steve Marshall; Dan Matthews; Laura Mellor; Esta Mion-Jones; Clare Mitchell; Rebecca Moisan; Steve Newell; Tom Proctor; Stuart Rodda; Charlotte Scott-Beveridge; Ambrose Scott-Moncrieff; Helen Simpson; Karen Wardley; Jessica Whitfield.